SOLA SCRIPTURA TOPICAL BIBLE™

What Does The Bible Say About

ANGELS

I0567823

SOLA SCRIPTURA TOPICAL BIBLE™

What Does The Bible Say About
ANGELS

Featuring the text of the **New American Standard Bible (NASB)**

Compiled by: Daniel John

Smart Publishing Ltd.
Surrey, British Columbia   Canada

Sola Scriptura Topical Bible:
What Does The Bible Say About Angels?

* A Chapter reprinted from the *Sola Scriptura Topical Bible* *

First Edition   Ingram 1.0 - *2022*

ISBN 978-1-988271-66-8

Copyright © 2020

Smart Publishing Ltd.
Surrey, British Columbia   Canada
synopticgospel.com

Compiled by: Daniel John
Cover design: Daniel John

All the verses and most of the included content is reprinted from
Sola Scriptura Topical Bible © 2009, 2017 by Smart Publishing Ltd.

Sola Scriptura Topical Bible is a rebranding of
Bible-Light: Understanding Spiritual Symbols © 2007,
which was originally published as *Bible-Chop* © 2005.

Printed by IngramSpark.

*   *   *   *   *

Sola Scriptura: Angels - PDF: ISBN 978-1-988271-62-0
Kindle: ISBN 978-1-988271-65-1

Other books in the *Sola Scriptura* Topical series:
What Does The Bible Say About Healing?   ISBN 978-1-988271-72-9
What Does The Bible Say About Prayer?   ISBN 978-1-988271-78-1
What Does The Bible Say About The Sabbath?   ISBN 978-1-988271-60-6

Sola Scriptura Topical Bible: Top 20 Spiritual Symbols
Paperback: ISBN 978-1-988271-85-9
PDF: ISBN 978-1-988271-17-0

Available at: solascriptura.ca

TABLE OF CONTENTS

                                                    Page

Foreword   i

Introduction   ii

Notes on Reading This Book   v

   1. Reading the Concordant Texts   vi

   2. Topic Header   viii

   3. Types of Keywords   ix

     3 A Inclusion Exception   x

     3 B Keyword Phrase Variation   xi

     The Books of *The Bible*   xii

The Concordant Texts

The Old Testament   1

The New Testament   36

     Other Titles in this Series   71

*The fear of the Lord is the beginning of **wisdom**,
and the **knowledge** of the Holy One is **understanding**.*

*All Scripture is given by inspiration of God,
and is profitable for doctrine, for reproof, for correction,
for instruction in righteousness;
that the man of God may be complete,
thoroughly equipped for every good work.*

2 Timothy 3:16-17

Dedicated to All who Love The Word of God.

FOREWORD

Welcome, to a powerful new way to understand the meaning and the message of the *Holy Bible!*

The **Sola Scriptura Topical Bible** was created to highlight and focus the important symbols that God has used to convey His message to us in *The Holy Bible*. Knowing what *The Bible* itself says about different topics is achieved by reading every verse of Scripture that mentions the topical theme in full context. By reading all of the related verses in order, a unique perspective and understanding is gained about what *The Bible* itself says about various important spiritual symbols and topical themes.

As **Sola Scriptura** means by *the Scriptures Alone* the Biblical verses are presented in this book without commentary or additional notes, beyond a basic dictionary definition of the keywords that define the topical theme.

Note to this Edition

While this edition of the **Sola Scriptura Topical Bible** focuses on a single topical theme, other popular spiritual topics are available in this series, including: *Angels*, *Faith*, *Healing*, *Prayer*, *The Church*, *Miracles*, *The Holy Spirit*, and more.

Comprehensive versions of *The Sola Scriptura Topical Bible* are available which include multiple spiritual themes as chapters:

★ **Sola Scriptura: Major Symbols**   - 56 Topical Chapters

★ **Sola Scriptura: Top 20 Spiritual Symbols**   - 20 Chapters

Look for these titles in your local bookstore, or on Amazon, and at *synopticgospel.com*.

INTRODUCTION

Since our beginning, humanity has searched for the meaning of this earthly life. Many people believe that God has created mankind on the earth to know Him, and to worship Him.

As the creator and educator of humanity, God who is Spirit (*John 4:24*) has communicated a message of spiritual guidance to us, using the physical things of this world as symbols that the human mind can understand.

Many people believe that God's guidance can be found within the Scriptures of *The Holy Bible*.

> *"You search the Scriptures, because you think that*
> *in them you have eternal life..."*   ~ *Jesus Christ (John 5:39)*

Understanding *The Bible* (Latin: *biblios* - meaning "little books") can be challenging because *The Bible* is actually two different covenants, in two different languages, in two sets of books, that have been bound together as a single volume for almost two millennia.

The Latin word *testament* means *covenant*, and these two covenants are known as the **Tanakh**, or the **Old Testament**, and the **New Testament**, or the Christian covenant. In most modern translations of *The Bible* there are 39 little books in the Old Testament, and 27 books in the New Testament, for a total of 66 books in a standard Protestant *Bible*.

Together, the 66 *little books* of *The Bible* were written by some forty men, over a period of more than 1,600 years, in three different languages (Hebrew, Aramaic & Greek). So what do the 750,000 words of *The Bible* say, and how can the meaning of this long and complex spiritual message be understood?

One way to know the message that is contained within the words of *The Bible* is to study the physical and spiritual symbols and themes that it mentions, such as *angels*, *Heaven*, *miracles* and *The Holy Spirit*. To see everything that *The Bible* says about a theme or topic it is necessary to read all of the Scriptures in *The Bible* that mention it. For this purpose a Concordance is useful to show the location (*chapter & verse*) of all of the occurrences of a topical keyword.

However, a *Concordance* lists only the *chapter* and the *verse* that contains the topical keyword, and you must then flip through a *Bible* to find and read that verse, and all of the verses that contain the same keyword.

In order to understand the full context of how a topical keyword is used in Scripture it is usually also necessary to read the verses that appear immediately before and after the verse that contains the keyword itself. Going back and forth from a list of references in a *Concordance* to look up each verse in a *Bible* is time-consuming and confusing, especially for large and complex topics where there are many occurrences of the keyword.

So that one can quickly and easily read all of the verses that mention a topical keyword, this book displays all of the verses associated with the topic in full context, and in the same order as they appear in *The Bible*.

Reading all of the verses that relate to a spiritual topic in sequence allows one to quickly know everything that *The Bible* itself says about the topic, and with this in mind it is possible to weigh the information and arrive at a point of personal truth and understanding about the meaning of those words.

> "… *line upon line, line upon line;*
> *here a little, there a little.*"   *Isaiah 28:10 & 13*

While not all of the Scriptures provided within this book may be necessary to fully understand the meaning of the topical theme, every related verse has been included so that what *The Bible* itself says about the topic is complete. As a study tool, the reader can mark or highlight for future reference those passages that are of personal importance or interest.

As for the title of this work, *Sola Scriptura* is a Latin term which means "the Scriptures alone" or, "only the Scriptures". *Sola Scriptura* is one of the *solae* (or *solas*) that were among the primary foundational doctrines of the reformers of the 16th century Catholic Church, as popularized by the German priest turned protestant, Martin Luther.

In addition to *Sola Scriptura*, the other two essential *solas* of the Protestant Reformation were *Sola Fide* - Faith Alone (that salvation is through faith in Jesus Christ alone) and *Sola Gratia* - Grace Alone (that salvation is by the grace of God alone).

The later additions of *Solus Christus* - Christ Alone (Jesus Christ alone is our Lord, Savior, and King), and *Soli Deo Gloria* - to the Glory of God Alone (that we live for the Glory of God alone), brought the number of fundamental *Solae* to five.

Sola Scriptura means that the *Scripture* of *The Bible* alone is the highest and final authority on all matters that deal with salvation. For the reformers, this meant that each person should read the words of God for themselves, and in their own language (not Latin), to see what *The Bible* itself says, and to be inspired by the Holy Spirit of God for the interpretation of the meaning of those words. This meant to not be overly influenced or controlled by the man-made interpretations, doctrines, and traditions of any particular church, even the Catholic Church.

As *Sola Scriptura* means by *the Scriptures alone,* the Scriptures included within this book appear in the same order as a standard Protestant *Bible* of 66 books, and beyond standard dictionary definitions, they are presented without additional notes or commentary.

As this work contains only the verses of the Scriptures, other additional resources should be consulted to gain a deeper understanding of what each topical symbol means, or spiritual theme represents. The search for additional meaning should begin with an examination of the origins of each topical keyword in its original language(s) using a *Lexicon*, an *Interlinear* and a *Dictionary*. Other resources that help to increase our understanding of the meaning of the topical keywords include a *Bible Concordance*, a *Bible Commentary*, and a *Biblical Encyclopedia*.

As for the meaning of the spiritual message of *The Bible*, the more that the themes found within the Scriptures are read and studied the greater one's understanding of the Word of God will grow to be.

May the Holy Spirit of God Guide us
to Understand His Holy Word!

Daniel John

July, 2020

solascriptura.ca

NOTES ON READING THIS BOOK

All of the verses included in this book are reprinted from the **New American Standard Bible (NASB)** translation of The Holy Scriptures. For more information about the NASB Edition of The Bible visit *lockman.org*.

This section of notes provides the methodology that was used to define the topical theme of this book, and it provides information about how the selection of included verses was made.

In this book the following terms are used:

Keyword	A word that identifies a spiritual topic or theme. *(see page ix)*
Keyword Phrase	A **keyword** that consists of two or more words.

Verse	A verse from *The Bible*; a line of Scripture.
Concordant Text	A verse, or series of consecutive verses, from a book of *The Bible*, that usually includes a **keyword** or **keyword phrase**. "Concordant" means that all of the provided verses are discussing the same topical theme.
	Most concordant texts include additional lines of scripture before and/or after the verse that includes a **keyword**. These additional verses provide sufficient context to understand the use and meaning of the topical keyword or symbol.

For more information on using this book see the following Notes:

Section		Page
1.	Reading the Concordant Texts	vi
2.	Topic Header	viii
3.	Types of Keywords	ix
	3A Inclusion Exception	x
	3B Keyword Phrase Variation	xi

1. READING THE CONCORDANT TEXTS

A *concordant text* is a verse or a series of consecutive verses from a book of *The Bible*, that usually contains a topical **keyword** or **keyword phrase**. The included concordant texts are all related to the same topic or theme, which in this book is *The Sabbath*.

Generally, every Scriptural occurrence of a topical keyword has been included within the provided concordant texts, along with any other related keywords that have the same meaning; such derivatives may include a keyword's English root, such as nouns, verbs, adjectives, and adverbs, etc. For example, the chapter titled **Believe** from the larger Topical Bible includes the tertiary keywords *believes*, *believing*, and *believed*. For more information on the types of keywords (main, secondary, tertiary) see page i*x*.

Occasionally, the scriptural occurrence of a listed keyword was not included within the provided set of concordant texts; for more information on *Inclusion Exceptions* see page *x*.

The verses contained in this book are reprinted from the **New American Standard Edition (NASB)** of *The Holy Bible*.

NOTES on Reading The Concordant Texts:

1. The concordant texts of this book appear in the same order as most *Bibles*, beginning with the *Book of Genesis* in the Old Testament, and ending with the *Book of Revelation* in the New Testament.

2. For easy identification, the topical keywords that appear within each set of concordant texts are highlighted in **bold** font.

3. *The Bible* chapter and verse reference for each set of concordant texts is listed at the end of the set of concordant verses. Use this reference to locate these verses in a standard *Bible*.

4. The length of the included Scriptures in each set of concordant texts has been edited to provide sufficient context to understand the use and the meaning of the topical keyword or keyword phrase. For additional context, use the Scripture reference to find the verses in a standard *Bible*.

5. Curly braces { } are sometimes included at the beginning of a set of concordant verses to identify the speaker where the name of the speaker does not appear within the provided verses.

Symbols Used within The Concordant Texts:

The following symbols provide additional information about the verses that are included within the provided sets of concordant texts.

~   Indicates that the end of a long *Bible* verse has been omitted because it does not directly contribute to understanding the use or meaning of the symbol. The omitted portion of a verse is cut off after either a comma, a colon, a semicolon, or a period.

> Paul, an **apostle** (not sent from men nor through the agency of man, but through Jesus Christ and God the Father, who raised Him from the dead), **~**
> *Galatians 1:1*

...   This indicates that the middle part of a long series of verses has been omitted because the verses do not contribute to understanding the topical theme of the chapter. The missing verses are indicated by ... ... within the concordant texts, and by ... within the scriptural reference. Use this reference to locate the omitted verses.

> They cast lots and the lot fell on Jonah. ...
>   ... So they picked up Jonah, threw him into the sea, and the sea stopped its raging.
> *Jonah 1:7...15*

<list>   Indicates that the middle of a series of verses that form a long
>   list has been omitted from the provided concordant texts.
       The missing verses are indicated by ..<list>.. and the missing part of the list is indicated by **>** within the scriptural reference for the concordant set. Use this reference to locate the omitted verses in a Bible.

> The record of the genealogy of Jesus the **Messiah**, the son of David, the son of Abraham: Abraham was the father of Isaac, Isaac the father of Jacob, and Jacob the father of Judah and his brothers.
>   Judah was the father of Perez and Zerah by Tamar, Perez was the father of Hezron, and Hezron the father of Ram. **..<list>..** Eliud was the father of Eleazar, Eleazar the father of Matthan, and Matthan the father of Jacob. Jacob was the father of Joseph the husband of Mary, by whom Jesus was born, who is called the **Messiah**.
> *Matthew 1:1-3 > 15-16*

2. TOPIC HEADER

This book includes a header that details information about the symbolic theme and topic of the book, and it identifies the keywords that are included within the provided concordant texts.

The header consists of two parts:

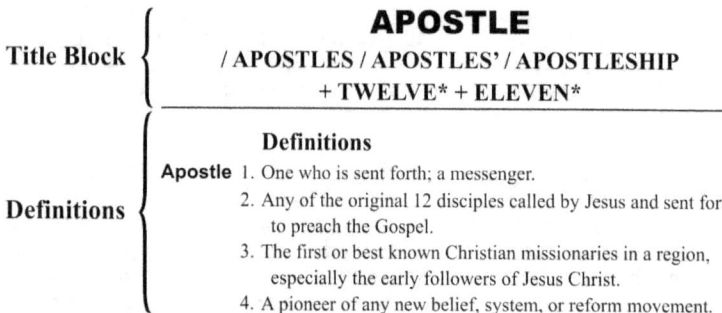

Title Block {

APOSTLE
/ APOSTLES / APOSTLES' / APOSTLESHIP
+ TWELVE* + ELEVEN*

Definitions {

Definitions

Apostle 1. One who is sent forth; a messenger.
2. Any of the original 12 disciples called by Jesus and sent forth to preach the Gospel.
3. The first or best known Christian missionaries in a region, especially the early followers of Jesus Christ.
4. A pioneer of any new belief, system, or reform movement.

Title Block

The title block identifies the topical theme of the book and it lists all of the keywords and keyword phrases that are included within the provided concordant texts. For more information on the different types of keywords see the following page.

Definitions

Basic dictionary definitions and meanings are provided for some of the keywords that are listed in the title block. For additional definitions, please refer to a dictionary, lexicon or Biblical dictionary.

3. TYPES OF KEYWORDS

The Title Block identifies the topical keywords and keyword phrases that have been included in the concordant texts of this book, along with other forms and variations of the keyword.

---

1. **Main Keyword**   (*Chapter Title*)

   This **keyword** or **keyword phrase** is the title of the book and it defines the symbol that is the starting point for compiling the list of topically related keywords.

2. **Secondary Keyword**   *symbol +*

   This keyword or keyword phrase is closely related or similar in meaning to the **main keyword**, but it does not share its root in English.

3. **Tertiary Keyword**   *symbol /*

   This keyword shares the same English root as the keyword that proceeds it in the list of keywords. Tertiary keywords are other forms of the **main** or **secondary** keyword that proceeds it in the list, and can include nouns, verbs, adjectives, and adverbs, etc.

---

1. Main Keyword *(Chapter Title)*

3. Tertiary Keyword

2. Secondary Keyword

ANGEL
/ ANGELS / ANGEL'S / ANGELIC / ARCHANGEL
+ HOLY ONE* / HOLY ONES + SONS OF GOD^

Inclusion Exception   *Keyword Phrase Variation*

---

* Inclusion Exception

Indicates that not all of the Biblical occurrences of the keyword or keyword phrase have been included in the concordant texts of this book. For more information about omitted keywords please see section *3 A.* on the following page.

∧ Keyword Phrase Variation

Indicates the individual words that make up a keyword phrase may appear in a variety of arrangements. For more information please see section *3 B.* on page *xvii.*

3A. INCLUSION EXCEPTION   Symbol: *

An **inclusion exception** is the term that identifies a keyword or keyword phrase in the Title Block for which every scriptural occurrence has not been included in the concordant texts of the chapter. If the keyword or keyword phrase does not have a * to the right of it then all of the related scriptures containing the keyword, as found in the NASB version of *The Bible*, have been included within the provided concordant texts of this book.

There are two types of inclusion exceptions:

1. The keyword has two (or more) different meanings

Some words have more than one distinct meaning, and in such cases only those occurrences of the keyword in the Scriptures that are topically related to the symbolic theme have been included in this book.

An example is in the chapter entitled **Fasting** which includes the keyword "fast". The word "fast" can refer several things, such as quickness and speed, or to hold something firmly (*to hold fast*), as well as the abstinence from eating food, as in "fasting". For the purposes of this book, only those scriptural occurrences of the word "fast", as in fasting; to abstain from food, have been included in the concordant texts of the chapter on **Fasting**.

2. The keyword has both a physical meaning and also a spiritually symbolic connotation

Some words have many definitions and meanings, as both a literal, physical, earthly or secular meaning, and also a distinctly different symbolic meaning and use as a concept, where the word metaphorically refers to something non-physical or "spiritual".

Generally, where a keyword can represent something both physical and also something purely spiritual or symbolic, only those occurrences of the keyword that are of spiritual significance to the symbolic theme have been included.

An example is the chapter titled **Kingdom*** where the word "kingdom" is used in *The Bible* with reference to the physical kingdoms that are the nations and countries of the earth, and also to the spiritual "Kingdom" that represents Heaven, God, or the church, etc. For the purposes of this book, references to the physical nations of the earth, such as the kingdoms of Israel, Judah, Babylon, and Assyria, etc. were not included within the provided concordant texts of the topic **Kingdom***.

3B. KEYWORD PHRASE VARIATION   Symbol: ∧

Sometimes in scripture the group of words that form a keyword phrase can include additional words that provide further descriptive meaning.

An example is the chapter titled **Son of God**^ which includes other variations of the keyword phrase such as the "**Son of** the living **God**" and the "**Son of** the Most High **God**", etc. In a few cases, the sequence of the individual words that make a keyword phrase can also appear in a rearranged order, as "**God's Son**".

Where a keyword phrase has a variety of possible word additions, all combinations and forms of the keyword phrase, as found in the NASB edition of The Bible, have generally been included in the provided concordant texts although not all of the additional derivatives and combinations of the keyword phrase have been specifically listed in the title block.

The presence of multiple word combinations and variations of a keyword phrase in the concordant texts is indicated by a ^ to the right of the listing of the keyword phrase in the title block, as in **Son of God**^.

~ End of Notes ~

THE BOOKS OF THE BIBLE

OLD TESTAMENT - THE HEBREW COVENANT

1. Genesis
2. Exodus
3. Leviticus
4. Numbers
5. Deuteronomy
6. Joshua
7. Judges
8. Ruth
9. I Samuel
10. II Samuel
11. I Kings
12. II Kings
13. I Chronicles
14. II Chronicles
15. Ezra
16. Nehemiah
17. Esther
18. Job
19. Psalms
20. Proverbs
21. Ecclesiastes
22. Song of Solomon
23. Isaiah
24. Jeremiah
25. Lamentations
26. Ezekiel
27. Daniel
28. Hosea
29. Joel
30. Amos
31. Obadiah
32. Jonah
33. Micah
34. Nahum
35. Habakkuk
36. Zephaniah
37. Haggai
38. Zechariah
39. Malachi

NEW TESTAMENT - THE CHRISTIAN COVENANT

1. Matthew
2. Mark
3. Luke
4. John
5. Acts
6. Romans
7. I Corinthians
8. II Corinthians
9. Galatians
10. Ephesians
11. Philippians
12. Colossians
13. I Thessalonians
14. II Thessalonians
15. I Timothy
16. II Timothy
17. Titus
18. Philemon
19. Hebrews
20. James
21. I Peter
22. II Peter
23. I John
24. II John
25. III John
26. Jude
27. Revelation

The
CONCORDANT
TEXTS

ANGELS

/ ANGEL / ANGEL'S / ANGELIC / ARCHANGEL
+ HOLY ONE* / HOLY ONES + SONS OF GOD^
+ CHERUB* / CHERUBIM* + SERAPHIM
+ STAR* / STARS*

Definitions

Angel
1. A messenger, specially of God.
2. One of a class of spiritual beings who act as attendants to God.
3. Divine members of the Heavenly assembly.
4. The dwellers of Paradise or Heaven.
5. An attendant or guardian spirit.
6. A representation of such a being, in human form, often with wings.
7. A deceased person whose soul is regarded as having been accepted into heaven.
8. A person having qualities that are generally attributed to an angel, such as beauty, purity, kindliness, charity or holiness.

Angelic
1. Resembling, relating to or proceeding from angels.
2. Having or appearing to have the characteristics or qualities of an angel; heavenly, saintly, holy, etc.

Archangel   A chief or principal angel.

Holy Ones   Divine members of God's heavenly assembly.

Sons of God
1. Divine members of God's heavenly assembly.
2. A reference in the Bible that can denote stars or angels.

Cherub / Cherubim
1. A lower order of winged angelic beings that attends or serves God; described as having four "faces" of three animals and also human.
2. Moderns depictions are of small, chubby, childlike figures with one set of wings.

Seraphim
1. A high order angelic being that serves God and attends His presence and His throne.
2. An attendant of God composed of flame or fire, and with two or three pairs of wings.

Star / Stars 1. A reference in the Bible that can denote angels. *(Revelation)*

OLD TESTAMENT

The Lord God said, "Behold, the man has become like one of Us, knowing good and evil; and now, he might stretch out his hand, and take also from the tree of life, and eat, and live forever" - therefore the Lord God sent him out from the garden of Eden, to cultivate the ground from which he was taken.

So He drove the man out; and at the east of the garden of Eden He stationed the **cherubim** and the flaming sword which turned every direction to guard the way to the tree of life.   *Genesis 3:22-24*

It came about, when men began to multiply on the face of the land, and daughters were born to them, that the **sons of God** saw that the daughters of men were beautiful; and they took wives for themselves, whomever they chose.

Then the Lord said, "My Spirit shall not strive with man forever, because he also is flesh; nevertheless his days shall be one hundred and twenty years."

The Nephilim were on the earth in those days, and also afterward, when the **sons of God** came in to the daughters of men, and they bore children to them. Those were the mighty men who were of old, men of renown.

Then the Lord saw that the wickedness of man was great on the earth, and that every intent of the thoughts of his heart was only evil continually. The Lord was sorry that He had made man on the earth, and He was grieved in His heart.

The Lord said, "I will blot out man whom I have created from the face of the land, from man to animals to creeping things and to birds of the sky; for I am sorry that I have made them."   *Genesis 6:1-7*

Sarai, Abram's wife had borne him no children, and she had an Egyptian maid whose name was Hagar. So Sarai said to Abram, "Now behold, the Lord has prevented me from bearing children. Please go in to my maid; perhaps I will obtain children through her."

And Abram listened to the voice of Sarai.

After Abram had lived ten years in the land of Canaan, Abram's wife Sarai took Hagar the Egyptian, her maid, and gave her to her huband Abram, as his wife.

He went in to Hagar, and she conceived; and when she saw that she had conceived, her mistress was despised in her sight.

And Sarai said to Abram, "May the wrong done me be upon you. I gave my maid into your arms, but when she saw that she had conceived, I was despised in her sight,

Genesis 16:1-13 > continued

May the Lord judge between and you and me."

But Abram said to Sarai, "Behold, your maid is in your power; do to her what is good in your sight." So Sarai treated her harshly, and she fled from her presence.

Now the **angel** of the Lord found her by a spring of water in the wilderness, by the spring on the way to Shur. He said, "Hagar, Sarai's maid, where have you come from and where are you going?"

And she said, "I am fleeing from the presence of my mistress Sarai."

Then the **angel** of the Lord said to her, "Return to your mistress, and submit yourself to her authority."

Moreover, the **angel** of the Lord said to her, "I will greatly multiply your descendants so that they will be too many to count."

The **angel** of the Lord said to her further, "Behold, you are with child, and you will bear a son; and you shall call his name Ishmael, because the Lord has given heed to your affliction. He will be a wild donkey of a man, his hand will be against everyone, and everyone's hand will be against him; and he will live to the east of all his brothers."

Then she called the name of the Lord who spoke to her, "You are a God who sees"; for she said, "Have I even remained alive here after seeing Him?" *Genesis 16:1-13*

Two **angels** came to Sodom in the evening as Lot was sitting in the gate of Sodom. When Lot saw them, he rose to meet them and bowed down with his face to the ground.

And he said, "Now behold, my lords, please turn aside into your servant's house, and spend the night, and wash your feet; then you may rise early and go on your way."

They said however, "No, but we shall spend the night in the square."

Yet he urged them strongly, so they turned aside to him and entered his house; and he prepared a feast for them, and baked unleavened bread, and they ate.

Before they lay down, the men of the city, the men of Sodom, surrounded the house, both young and old, all the people from every quarter; and they called to Lot and said to him, "Where are the men who came to you tonight? Bring them out to us that we may have relations with them."

But Lot went out to them at the doorway, and shut the door behind him, and said, "Please, my brothers, do not act wickedly. Now behold, I have two daughters who have not had relations with man; please let me bring them out to you, and do to them whatever you like; only do nothing to these men, inasmuch as they have come under the shelter of my roof."

But they said, "Stand aside." Furthermore, they said, "This one came in as an alien, and already he is acting like a judge; now we will treat you worse than them."

So they pressed hard against Lot and came near to break the door. But the men reached out their hands and brought Lot into the house with them, and shut the door.

They struck the men who were at the doorway of the house with blindness, both small and great, so that they wearied themselves trying to find the doorway.

Then the two men said to Lot, "Whom else have you here? A son-in-law, and your sons, and your daughters, and whomever you have in the city, bring them out of the place; for we are about to destroy this place, because their outcry has become so great before the Lord that the Lord has sent us to destroy it."

Lot went out and spoke to his sons-in-law, who were to marry his daughters, and said, "Up, get out of this place, for the Lord will destroy the city." But he appeared to his sons-in-law to be jesting.

When morning dawned, the **angels** urged Lot, saying, "Up, take your wife and your two daughters who are here, or you will be swept away in the punishment of the city."

But he hesitated. So the men seized his hand and the hand of his wife and the hands of his two daughters, for the compassion of the Lord was upon him; and they brought him out, and put him outside the city.

When they had brought them outside, one said, "Escape for your life! Do not look behind you, and do not stay anywhere in the valley; escape to the mountains, or you will be swept away."

But Lot said to them, "Oh no, my lords! Now behold, your servant has found favor in your sight, and you have magnified your lovingkind-ness, which you have shown me by saving my life; but I cannot escape to the mountains, for the disaster will overtake me and I will die; now behold, this town is near enough to flee to, and it is small. Please, let me escape there (is it not small?) that my life may be saved."

He said to him, "Behold, I grant you this request also, not to over-throw the town of which you have spoken. Hurry, escape there, for I cannot do anything until you arrive there." Therefore the name of the town was called Zoar.

The sun had risen over the earth when Lot came to Zoar. Then the Lord rained on Sodom and Gomorrah brimstone and fire from the Lord out of heaven, and He overthrew those cities, and all the valley, and all the inhabitants of the cities, and what grew on the ground.

But his wife, from behind him, looked back, and she became a pillar of salt. *Genesis 19:1-26*

Sarah saw the son of Hagar the Egyptian, whom she had borne to Abraham, mocking. Therefore she said to Abraham, "Drive out this maid and her son, for the son of this maid shall not be an heir with my son Isaac."

The matter distressed Abraham greatly because of his son. But God said to Abraham, "Do not be distressed because of the lad and your maid; whatever Sarah tells you, listen to her, for through Isaac your descendants shall be named.

"And of the son of the maid I will make a nation also, because he is your descendant."

So Abraham rose early in the morning and took bread and a skin of water and gave them to Hagar, putting them on her shoulder, and gave her the boy, and sent her away. And she departed and wandered about in the wilderness of Beersheba.

When the water in the skin was used up, she left the boy under one of the bushes. Then she went and sat down opposite him, about a bowshot away, for she said, "Do not let me see the boy die."

And she sat opposite him, and lifted up her voice and wept.

God heard the lad crying; and the **angel** of God called to Hagar from heaven and said to her, "What is the matter with you, Hagar? Do not fear, for God has heard the voice of the lad where he is.

"Arise, lift up the lad, and hold him by the hand, for I will make a great nation of him."

Then God opened her eyes and she saw a well of water; and she went and filled the skin with water and gave the lad a drink.

God was with the lad, and he grew; and he lived in the wilderness and became an archer. He lived in the wilderness of Paran, and his mother took a wife for him from the land of Egypt. *Genesis 21:9-21*

It came about after these things, that God tested Abraham, and said to him, "Abraham!"

And he said, "Here I am."

He said, "Take now your son, your only son, whom you love, Isaac, and go to the land of Moriah, and offer him there as a burnt offering on one of the mountains of which I will tell you."

So Abraham rose early in the morning and saddled his donkey, and took two of his young men with him and Isaac his son; and he split wood for the burnt offering, and arose and went to the place of which God had told him.

On the third day, Abraham raised his eyes and saw the place from a distance. Abraham said to his young men, "Stay here with the donkey, and I and the lad will go over there; and we will worship and return to you."

Abraham took the wood of the burnt offering and laid it on Isaac his son, and he took in his hand the fire and the knife. So the two of them walked on together.

Isaac spoke to Abraham his father and said, "My father!" And he said, "Here I am, my son."

And he said, "Behold, the fire and the wood, but where is the lamb for the burnt offering?"

Abraham said, "God will provide for Himself the lamb for the burnt offering, my son." So the two of them walked on together.

Then they came to the place of which God had told him; and Abraham built the altar there and arranged the wood, and bound his son Isaac and laid him on the altar, on top of the wood.

Abraham stretched out his hand and took the knife to slay his son. But the **angel** of the Lord called to him from heaven and said, "Abraham, Abraham!"

And he said, "Here I am."

He said, "Do not stretch out your hand against the lad, and do nothing to him; for now I know that you fear God, since you have not withheld your son, your only son, from Me."

Then Abraham raised his eyes and looked, and behold, behind him a ram caught in the thicket by his horns; and Abraham went and took the ram and offered him up for a burnt offering in the place of his son.

Abraham called the name of that place The Lord Will Provide, as it is said to this day, "In the mount of the Lord it will be provided."

Then the **angel** of the Lord called to Abraham a second time from heaven, and said, "By Myself I have sworn, declares the Lord, because you have done this thing and have not withheld your son, your only son, indeed I will greatly bless you, and I will greatly multiply your seed as the stars of the heavens and as the sand which is on the seashore; and your seed shall possess the gate of their enemies.

"In your seed all the nations of the earth shall be blessed, because you have obeyed My voice." *Genesis 22:1-18*

Abraham was old, advanced in age; and the Lord had blessed Abraham in every way.

Abraham said to his servant, the oldest of his household, who had charge of all that he owned, "Please place your hand under my thigh, and I will make you swear by the Lord, the God of heaven and the God of earth, that you shall not take a wife for my son from the daughters of the Canaanites, among whom I live, but you will go to my country and to my relatives, and take a wife for my son Isaac."

The servant said to him, "Suppose the woman is not willing to follow me to this land; should I take your son back to the land from where you came?" *Genesis 24:1-9 > continued*

Then Abraham said to him, "Beware that you do not take my son back there! The Lord, the God of heaven, who took me from my father's house and from the land of my birth, and who spoke to me and who swore to me, saying, 'To your descendants I will give this land,' He will send His **angel** before you, and you will take a wife for my son from there.

"But if the woman is not willing to follow you, then you will be free from this my oath; only do not take my son back there."

So the servant placed his hand under the thigh of Abraham his master, and swore to him concerning this matter.   > *Genesis 24:1-9*

My master made me swear, saying, "You shall not take a wife for my son from the daughters of the Canaanites, in whose land I live; but you shall go to my father's house and to my relatives, and take a wife for my son."

I said to my master, "Suppose the woman does not follow me."

He said to me, "The Lord, before whom I have walked, will send His **angel** with you to make your journey successful, and you will take a wife for my son from my relatives and from my father's house: Then you will be free from my oath, when you come to my relatives; and if they do not give her to you, you will be free from my oath."

Genesis 24:37-41

Jacob departed from Beersheba and went toward Haran. He came to a certain place and spent the night there, because the sun had set; and he took one of the stones of the place and put it under his head, and lay down in that place.

He had a dream, and behold, a ladder was set on the earth with its top reaching to heaven; and behold, the **angels** of God were ascending and descending on it.

And behold, the Lord stood above it and said, "I am the Lord, the God of your father Abraham and the God of Isaac; the land on which you lie, I will give it to you and to your descendants. Your descendants will also be like the dust of the earth, and you will spread out to the west and to the east and to the north and to the south; and in you and in your descendants shall all the families of the earth be blessed.

"Behold, I am with you and will keep you wherever you go, and will bring you back to this land; for I will not leave you until I have done what I have promised you."

Then Jacob awoke from his sleep and said, "Surely the Lord is in this place, and I did not know it."

He was afraid and said, "How awesome is this place! This is none other than the house of God, and this is the gate of heaven."

So Jacob rose early in the morning, and took the stone that he had put under his head and set it up as a pillar and poured oil on its top. He called the name of that place Bethel; however, previously the name of the city had been Luz.   *Genesis 28:10-19*

It came about at the time when the flock were mating that I lifted up my eyes and saw in a dream, and behold, the male goats which were mating were striped, speckled, and mottled.

Then the **angel** of God said to me in the dream, "Jacob," and I said, "Here I am."

He said, "Lift up now your eyes and see that all the male goats which are mating are striped, speckled, and mottled; for I have seen all that Laban has been doing to you.

"I am the God of Bethel, where you anointed a pillar, where you made a vow to Me; now arise, leave this land, and return to the land of your birth."   *Genesis 31:10-13*

As Jacob went on his way, the **angels** of God met him.

Jacob said when he saw them, "This is God's camp."   So he named that place Mahanaim.   *Genesis 32:1-2*

The eyes of Israel were so dim from age that he could not see. Then Joseph brought them close to him, and he kissed them and embraced them.

Israel said to Joseph, "I never expected to see your face, and behold, God has let me see your children as well."   Then Joseph took them from his knees, and bowed with his face to the ground.

Joseph took them both, Ephraim with his right hand toward Israel's left, and Manasseh with his left hand toward Israel's right, and brought them close to him.

But Israel stretched out his right hand and laid it on the head of Ephraim, who was the younger, and his left hand on Manasseh's head, crossing his hands, although Manasseh was the firstborn.

He blessed Joseph, and said, "The God before whom my fathers Abraham and Isaac walked, the God who has been my shepherd all my life to this day, the **angel** who has redeemed me from all evil, bless the lads; and may my name live on in them, and the names of my fathers Abraham and Isaac; and may they grow into a multitude in the midst of the earth."   *Genesis 48:10-16*

Moses was pasturing the flock of Jethro his father-in-law, the priest of Midian; and he led the flock to the west side of the wilderness and came to Horeb, the mountain of God.

The **angel** of the Lord appeared to him in a blazing fire from the

Exodus 3:1-11 > continued

midst of a bush; and he looked, and behold, the bush was burning with fire, yet the bush was not consumed.

So Moses said, "I must turn aside now and see this marvelous sight, why the bush is not burned up."

When the Lord saw that he turned aside to look, God called to him from the midst of the bush and said, "Moses, Moses!"

And he said, "Here I am."

Then He said, "Do not come near here; remove your sandals from your feet, for the place on which you are standing is holy ground."

He said also, "I am the God of your father, the God of Abraham, the God of Isaac, and the God of Jacob."

Then Moses hid his face, for he was afraid to look at God.

The Lord said, "I have surely seen the affliction of My people who are in Egypt, and have given heed to their cry because of their task-masters, for I am aware of their sufferings. So I have come down to deliver them from the power of the Egyptians, and to bring them up from that land to a good and spacious land, to a land flowing with milk and honey, to the place of the Canaanite and the Hittite and the Amo-rite and the Perizzite and the Hivite and the Jebusite.

"Now, behold, the cry of the sons of Israel has come to Me; further-more, I have seen the oppression with which the Egyptians are oppres-sing them. Therefore, come now, and I will send you to Pharaoh, so that you may bring My people, the sons of Israel, out of Egypt."

But Moses said to God, "Who am I, that I should go to Pharaoh, and that I should bring the sons of Israel out of Egypt?"

And He said, "Certainly I will be with you, and this shall be the sign to you that it is I who have sent you: when you have brought the people out of Egypt, you shall worship God at this mountain."   > *Exodus 3:1-11*

The Lord said to Moses, "Why are you crying out to Me? Tell the sons of Israel to go forward. As for you, lift up your staff and stretch out your hand over the sea and divide it, and the sons of Israel shall go through the midst of the sea on dry land.

"As for Me, behold, I will harden the hearts of the Egyptians so that they will go in after them; and I will be honored through Pharaoh and all his army, through his chariots and his horsemen. Then the Egyptians will know that I am the Lord, when I am honored through Pharaoh, through his chariots and his horsemen."

The **angel** of God, who had been going before the camp of Israel, moved and went behind them; and the pillar of cloud moved from be-fore them and stood behind them. So it came between the camp of Egypt and the camp of Israel; and there was the cloud along with the darkness, yet it gave light at night. Thus the one did not come near the other all night.

Then Moses stretched out his hand over the sea; and the Lord swept the sea back by a strong east wind all night and turned the sea into dry land, so the waters were divided.   *Exodus 14:15-21*

{The Lord said to Moses,} "Behold, I am going to send an **angel** before you to guard you along the way and to bring you into the place which I have prepared. Be on your guard before him and obey his voice; do not be rebellious toward him, for he will not pardon your transgression, since My name is in him.

"But if you truly obey his voice and do all that I say, then I will be an enemy to your enemies and an adversary to your adversaries. For My **angel** will go before you and bring you in to the land of the Amorites, the Hittites, the Perizzites, the Canaanites, the Hivites and the Jebusites; and I will completely destroy them.

"You shall not worship their gods, nor serve them, nor do according to their deeds; but you shall utterly overthrow them and break their sacred pillars in pieces. But you shall serve the Lord your God, and He will bless your bread and your water; and I will remove sickness from your midst."   *Exodus 23:20-25*

Moses returned to the Lord, and said, "Alas, this people has committed a great sin, and they have made a god of gold for themselves. But now, if You will, forgive their sin - and if not, please blot me out from Your book which You have written!"

The Lord said to Moses, "Whoever has sinned against Me, I will blot him out of My book. But go now, lead the people where I told you. Behold, My **angel** shall go before you; nevertheless in the day when I punish, I will punish them for their sin."

Then the Lord smote the people, because of what they did with the calf which Aaron had made.

Then the Lord spoke to Moses, "Depart, go up from here, you and the people whom you have brought up from the land of Egypt, to the land of which I swore to Abraham, Isaac, and Jacob, saying, 'To your descendants I will give it.'

"I will send an **angel** before you and I will drive out the Canaanite, the Amorite, the Hittite, the Perizzite, the Hivite and the Jebusite. Go up to a land flowing with milk and honey; for I will not go up in your midst, because you are an obstinate people, and I might destroy you on the way."

When the people heard this sad word, they went into mourning, and none of them put on his ornaments.   *Exodus 32:31 - 33:4*

From Kadesh Moses then sent messengers to the king of Edom: "Thus your brother Israel has said, 'You know all the hardship that has befallen us; that our fathers went down to Egypt, and we stayed in Egypt a long time, and the Egyptians treated us and our fathers badly. But when we cried out to the Lord, He heard our voice and sent an **angel** and brought us out from Egypt; now behold, we are at Kadesh, a town on the edge of your territory.

'Please let us pass through your land. We will not pass through field or through vineyard; we will not even drink water from a well. We will go along the king's highway, not turning to the right or left, until we pass through your territory.' "

Edom, however, said to him, "You shall not pass through us, or I will come out with the sword against you." *Numbers 20:14-18*

God came to Balaam at night and said to him, "If the men have come to call you, rise up and go with them; but only the word which I speak to you shall you do."

So Balaam arose in the morning, and saddled his donkey and went with the leaders of Moab. But God was angry because he was going, and the **angel** of the Lord took his stand in the way as an adversary against him.

Now he was riding on his donkey and his two servants were with him. When the donkey saw the **angel** of the Lord standing in the way with his drawn sword in his hand, the donkey turned off from the way and went into the field; but Balaam struck the donkey to turn her back into the way.

Then the **angel** of the Lord stood in a narrow path of the vineyards, with a wall on this side and a wall on that side. When the donkey saw the **angel** of the Lord, she pressed herself to the wall and pressed Balaam's foot against the wall, so he struck her again.

The **angel** of the Lord went further, and stood in a narrow place where there was no way to turn to the right hand or the left. When the donkey saw the **angel** of the Lord, she lay down under Balaam; so Balaam was angry and struck the donkey with his stick.

And the Lord opened the mouth of the donkey, and she said to Balaam, "What have I done to you, that you have struck me these three times?"

Then Balaam said to the donkey, "Because you have made a mockery of me! If there had been a sword in my hand, I would have killed you by now."

The donkey said to Balaam, "Am I not your donkey on which you have ridden all your life to this day? Have I ever been accustomed to do so to you?" And he said, "No."

Then the Lord opened the eyes of Balaam, and he saw the **angel** of the Lord standing in the way with his drawn sword in his hand; and he bowed all the way to the ground.

The **angel** of the Lord said to him, "Why have you struck your donkey these three times? Behold, I have come out as an adversary, because your way was contrary to me."

Balaam said to the **angel** of the Lord, "I have sinned, for I did not know that you were standing in the way against me. Now then, if it is displeasing to you, I will turn back."

But the **angel** of the Lord said to Balaam, "Go with the men, but you shall speak only the word which I tell you."

So Balaam went along with the leaders of Balak.   *Numbers 22:20-35*

This is the blessing with which Moses the man of God blessed the sons of Israel before his death.

He said, "The Lord came from Sinai, and dawned on them from Seir; He shone forth from Mount Paran, and He came from the midst of ten thousand **holy ones**; at His right hand there was flashing lightning for them. Indeed, He loves the people; all Your **holy ones** are in Your hand, and they followed in Your steps; everyone receives of Your words."   *Deuteronomy 33:1-3*

It came about when Joshua was by Jericho, that he lifted up his eyes and looked, and behold, a man was standing opposite him with his sword drawn in his hand, and Joshua went to him and said to him, "Are you for us or for our adversaries?"

He said, "No; rather I indeed come now as captain of the host of the Lord."

And Joshua fell on his face to the earth, and bowed down, and said to him, "What has my lord to say to his servant?"

The captain of the Lord's host said to Joshua, "Remove your sandals from your feet, for the place where you are standing is holy." And Joshua did so. Now Jericho was tightly shut because of the sons of Israel; no one went out and no one came in.

The Lord said to Joshua, "See, I have given Jericho into your hand, with its king and the valiant warriors. You shall march around the city, all the men of war circling the city once. You shall do so for six days. Also seven priests shall carry seven trumpets of rams' horns before the ark; then on the seventh day you shall march around the city seven times, and the priests shall blow the trumpets.

"It shall be that when they make a long blast with the ram's horn, and when you hear the sound of the trumpet, all the people shall shout with a great shout; and the wall of the city will fall down flat, and the people will go up every man straight ahead."   *Joshua 5:13 - 6:5*

The **angel** of the Lord came up from Gilgal to Bochim. And he said, "I brought you up out of Egypt and led you into the land which I have sworn to your fathers; and I said, 'I will never break My covenant with you, and as for you, you shall make no covenant with the inhabitants of this land; you shall tear down their altars.'

"But you have not obeyed Me; what is this you have done? Therefore I also said, 'I will not drive them out before you; but they will become as thorns in your sides and their gods will be a snare to you.' "

When the **angel** of the Lord spoke these words to all the sons of Israel, the people lifted up their voices and wept.

So they named that place Bochim; and there they sacrificed to the Lord. *Judges 2:1-5*

The **stars** fought from heaven, from their courses they fought against Sisera. The torrent of Kishon swept them away, the ancient torrent, the torrent Kishon. O my soul, march on with strength.

Then the horses' hoofs beat from the dashing, the dashing of his valiant steeds.

"Curse Meroz," said the **angel** of the Lord, "utterly curse its inhabitants; because they did not come to the help of the Lord, to the help of the Lord against the warriors." *Judges 5:20-23*

The **angel** of the Lord came and sat under the oak that was in Ophrah, which belonged to Joash the Abiezrite as his son Gideon was beating out wheat in the wine press in order to save it from the Midianites.

The **angel** of the Lord appeared to him and said to him, "The Lord is with you, O valiant warrior".

Then Gideon said to him, "O my lord, if the Lord is with us, why then has all this happened to us? And where are all His miracles which our fathers told us about, saying, 'Did not the Lord bring us up from Egypt?' But now the Lord has abandoned us and given us into the hand of Midian."

The Lord looked at him and said, "Go in this your strength and deliver Israel from the hand of Midian. Have I not sent you?"

He said to Him, "O Lord, how shall I deliver Israel? Behold, my family is the least in Manasseh, and I am the youngest in my father's house."

But the Lord said to him, "Surely I will be with you, and you shall defeat Midian as one man."

So Gideon said to Him, "If now I have found favor in Your sight, then show me a sign that it is You who speak with me. Please do not depart from here, until I come back to You, and bring out my offering and lay it before You."

And He said, "I will remain until you return."

Then Gideon went in and prepared a young goat and unleavened bread from an ephah of flour; he put the meat in a basket and the broth in a pot, and brought them out to him under the oak and presented them.

The **angel** of God said to him, "Take the meat and the unleavened bread and lay them on this rock, and pour out the broth." And he did so.

Then the **angel** of the Lord put out the end of the staff that was in his hand and touched the meat and the unleavened bread; and fire sprang up from the rock and consumed the meat and the unleavened bread. Then the **angel** of the Lord vanished from his sight.

When Gideon saw that he was the **angel** of the Lord, he said, "Alas, O Lord God! For now I have seen the **angel** of the Lord face to face."

The Lord said to him, "Peace to you, do not fear; you shall not die."

Then Gideon built an altar there to the Lord and named it The Lord is Peace. To this day it is still in Ophrah of the Abiezrites.   *Judges 6:11-24*

The sons of Israel again did evil in the sight of the Lord, so that the Lord gave them into the hands of the Philistines forty years. There was a certain man of Zorah, of the family of the Danites, whose name was Manoah; and his wife was barren and had borne no children.

Then the **angel** of the Lord appeared to the woman and said to her, "Behold now, you are barren and have borne no children, but you shall conceive and give birth to a son. Now therefore, be careful not to drink wine or strong drink, nor eat any unclean thing. For behold, you shall conceive and give birth to a son, and no razor shall come upon his head, for the boy shall be a Nazirite to God from the womb; and he shall begin to deliver Israel from the hands of the Philistines."

Then the woman came and told her husband, saying, "A man of God came to me and his appearance was like the appearance of the **angel** of God, very awesome. And I did not ask him where he came from, nor did he tell me his name. But he said to me, 'Behold, you shall conceive and give birth to a son, and now you shall not drink wine or strong drink nor eat any unclean thing, for the boy shall be a Nazirite to God from the womb to the day of his death.' "

Then Manoah entreated the Lord and said, "O Lord, please let the man of God whom You have sent come to us again that he may teach us what to do for the boy who is to be born."

God listened to the voice of Manoah; and the **angel** of God came again to the woman as she was sitting in the field, but Manoah her husband was not with her. So the woman ran quickly and told her husband, "Behold, the man who came the other day has appeared to me."

Judges 13:1-24 > continued

Then Manoah arose and followed his wife, and when he came to the man he said to him, "Are you the man who spoke to the woman?"

And he said, "I am."

Manoah said, "Now when your words come to pass, what shall be the boy's mode of life and his vocation?"

So the **angel** of the Lord said to Manoah, "Let the woman pay attention to all that I said. She should not eat anything that comes from the vine nor drink wine or strong drink, nor eat any unclean thing; let her observe all that I commanded."

Then Manoah said to the **angel** of the Lord, "Please let us detain you so that we may prepare a young goat for you."

The **angel** of the Lord said to Manoah, "Though you detain me, I will not eat your food, but if you prepare a burnt offering, then offer it to the Lord." For Manoah did not know that he was the **angel** of the Lord.

Manoah said to the **angel** of the Lord, "What is your name, so that when your words come to pass, we may honor you?"

But the **angel** of the Lord said to him, "Why do you ask my name, seeing it is wonderful?"

So Manoah took the young goat with the grain offering and offered it on the rock to the Lord, and He performed wonders while Manoah and his wife looked on. For it came about when the flame went up from the altar toward heaven, that the **angel** of the Lord ascended in the flame of the altar.

When Manoah and his wife saw this, they fell on their faces to the ground.

Now the **angel** of the Lord did not appear to Manoah or his wife again. Then Manoah knew that he was the **angel** of the Lord.

So Manoah said to his wife, "We will surely die, for we have seen God."

But his wife said to him, "If the Lord had desired to kill us, He would not have accepted a burnt offering and a grain offering from our hands, nor would He have shown us all these things, nor would He have let us hear things like this at this time."

Then the woman gave birth to a son and named him Samson; and the child grew up and the Lord blessed him.   > Judges 13:1-24

Achish called David and said to him, "As the Lord lives, you have been upright, and your going out and your coming in with me in the army are pleasing in my sight; for I have not found evil in you from the day of your coming to me to this day. Nevertheless, you are not pleasing in the sight of the lords. Now therefore return and go in peace, that you may not displease the lords of the Philistines."

David said to Achish, "But what have I done? And what have you found in your servant from the day when I came before you to this day, that I may not go and fight against the enemies of my lord the king?"

But Achish replied to David, "I know that you are pleasing in my sight, like an **angel** of God; nevertheless the commanders of the Philistines have said, 'He must not go up with us to the battle.' "

1 Samuel 29:6-9

Your maidservant said, "Please let the word of my lord the king be comforting, for as the **angel** of God, so is my lord the king to discern good and evil. And may the Lord your God be with you."

Then the king answered and said to the woman, "Please do not hide anything from me that I am about to ask you."

And the woman said, "Let my lord the king please speak."

So the king said, "Is the hand of Joab with you in all this?"

And the woman replied, "As your soul lives, my lord the king, no one can turn to the right or to the left from anything that my lord the king has spoken. Indeed, it was your servant Joab who commanded me, and it was he who put all these words in the mouth of your maidservant; in order to change the appearance of things your servant Joab has done this thing. But my lord is wise, like the wisdom of the **angel** of God, to know all that is in the earth."

Then the king said to Joab, "Behold now, I will surely do this thing; go therefore, bring back the young man Absalom."　　*2 Samuel 14:17-21*

So he answered, "O my lord, the king, my servant deceived me; for your servant said, 'I will saddle a donkey for myself that I may ride on it and go with the king,' because your servant is lame. Moreover, he has slandered your servant to my lord the king; but my lord the king is like the **angel** of God, therefore do what is good in your sight."

2 Samuel 19:26-27

In my distress I called upon the Lord, Yes, I cried to my God; and from His temple He heard my voice, and my cry for help came into His ears.

Then the earth shook and quaked, the foundations of heaven were trembling and were shaken, because He was angry. Smoke went up out of His nostrils, fire from His mouth devoured; coals were kindled by it.

He bowed the heavens also, and came down with thick darkness under His feet. And He rode on a **cherub** and flew; and He appeared on the wings of the wind. And He made darkness canopies around Him, a mass of waters, thick clouds of the sky.　　*2 Samuel 22:7-12*

David's heart troubled him after he had numbered the people. So David said to the Lord, "I have sinned greatly in what I have done. But now, O Lord, please take away the iniquity of Your servant, for I have acted very foolishly."　　*2 Samuel 24:10-19 > continued*

When David arose in the morning, the word of the Lord came to the prophet Gad, David's seer, saying, "Go and speak to David, 'Thus the Lord says, "I am offering you three things; choose for yourself one of them, which I will do to you."'"

So Gad came to David and told him, and said to him, "Shall seven years of famine come to you in your land? Or will you flee three months before your foes while they pursue you? Or shall there be three days' pestilence in your land? Now consider and see what answer I shall return to Him who sent me."

Then David said to Gad, "I am in great distress. Let us now fall into the hand of the Lord for His mercies are great, but do not let me fall into the hand of man."

So the Lord sent a pestilence upon Israel from the morning until the appointed time, and seventy thousand men of the people from Daniel to Beersheba died.

When the **angel** stretched out his hand toward Jerusalem to destroy it, the Lord relented from the calamity and said to the **angel** who destroyed the people, "It is enough! Now relax your hand!" And the **angel** of the Lord was by the threshing floor of Araunah the Jebusite.

Then David spoke to the Lord when he saw the **angel** who was striking down the people, and said, "Behold, it is I who have sinned, and it is I who have done wrong; but these sheep, what have they done? Please let Your hand be against me and against my father's house."

So Gad came to David that day and said to him, "Go up, erect an altar to the Lord on the threshing floor of Araunah the Jebusite."

David went up according to the word of Gad, just as the Lord had commanded. *2 Samuel 24:10-19*

An old prophet was living in Bethel; and his sons came and told him all the deeds which the man of God had done that day in Bethel; the words which he had spoken to the king, these also they related to their father.

Their father said to them, "Which way did he go?" Now his sons had seen the way which the man of God who came from Judah had gone.

Then he said to his sons, "Saddle the donkey for me." So they saddled the donkey for him and he rode away on it.

So he went after the man of God and found him sitting under an oak; and he said to him, "Are you the man of God who came from Judah?"

And he said, "I am."

Then he said to him, "Come home with me and eat bread."

He said, "I cannot return with you, nor go with you, nor will I eat bread or drink water with you in this place. For a command came to me by the word of the Lord, 'You shall eat no bread, nor drink water there; do not return by going the way which you came.' "

He said to him, "I also am a prophet like you, and an **angel** spoke to me by the word of the Lord, saying, 'Bring him back with you to your house, that he may eat bread and drink water.' "

But he lied to him. So he went back with him, and ate bread in his house and drank water.

Now it came about, as they were sitting down at the table, that the word of the Lord came to the prophet who had brought him back; and he cried to the man of God who came from Judah, saying, "Thus says the Lord, 'Because you have disobeyed the command of the Lord, and have not observed the commandment which the Lord your God commanded you, but have returned and eaten bread and drunk water in the place of which He said to you, "Eat no bread and drink no water"; your body shall not come to the grave of your fathers.' "

It came about after he had eaten bread and after he had drunk, that he saddled the donkey for him, for the prophet whom he had brought back.

Now when he had gone, a lion met him on the way and killed him, and his body was thrown on the road, with the donkey standing beside it; the lion also was standing beside the body. *1 Kings 13:11-24*

Ahab told Jezebel all that Elijah had done, and how he had killed all the prophets with the sword.

Then Jezebel sent a messenger to Elijah, saying, "So may the gods do to me and even more, if I do not make your life as the life of one of them by tomorrow about this time."

And he was afraid and arose and ran for his life and came to Beersheba, which belongs to Judah, and left his servant there. But he himself went a day's journey into the wilderness, and came and sat down under a juniper tree; and he requested for himself that he might die, and said, "It is enough; now, O Lord, take my life, for I am not better than my fathers."

He lay down and slept under a juniper tree; and behold, there was an **angel** touching him, and he said to him, "Arise, eat."

Then he looked and behold, there was at his head a bread cake baked on hot stones, and a jar of water. So he ate and drank and lay down again.

The **angel** of the Lord came again a second time and touched him and said, "Arise, eat, because the journey is too great for you."

So he arose and ate and drank, and went in the strength of that food forty days and forty nights to Horeb, the mountain of God.

1 Kings 19:1-8

Ahaziah fell through the lattice in his upper chamber which was in Samaria, and became ill. So he sent messengers and said to them, "Go, inquire of Baalzebub, the god of Ekron, whether I will recover from this sickness."

But the **angel** of the Lord said to Elijah the Tishbite, "Arise, go up to meet the messengers of the king of Samaria and say to them, 'Is it because there is no God in Israel that you are going to inquire of Baalzebub, the god of Ekron?' Now therefore thus says the Lord, 'You shall not come down from the bed where you have gone up, but you shall surely die.' "

Then Elijah departed. *2 Kings 1:2-4*

The **angel** of the Lord said to Elijah, "Go down with him; do not be afraid of him." So he arose and went down with him to the king.

Then he said to him, "Thus says the Lord, 'Because you have sent messengers to inquire of Baalzebub, the god of Ekron - is it because there is no God in Israel to inquire of His word? - therefore you shall not come down from the bed where you have gone up, but shall surely die.'"

So Ahaziah died according to the word of the Lord which Elijah had spoken. And because he had no son, Jehoram became king in his place in the second year of Jehoram the son of Jehoshaphat, king of Judah. *2 Kings 1:15-17*

Thus says the Lord concerning the king of Assyria, "He will not come to this city or shoot an arrow there; and he will not come before it with a shield or throw up a siege ramp against it. By the way that he came, by the same he will return, and he shall not come to this city," declares the Lord. "For I will defend this city to save it for My own sake and for My servant David's sake."

Then it happened that night that the **angel** of the Lord went out and struck 185,000 in the camp of the Assyrians; and when men rose early in the morning, behold, all of them were dead.

So Sennacherib king of Assyria departed and returned home, and lived at Nineveh. *2 Kings 19:32-36*

Satan stood up against Israel and moved David to number Israel. So David said to Joab and to the princes of the people, "Go, number Israel from Beersheba even to Dan, and bring me word that I may know their number."

Joab said, "May the Lord add to His people a hundred times as many as they are! But, my lord the king, are they not all my lord's servants? Why does my lord seek this thing? Why should he be a cause of guilt to Israel?"

Nevertheless, the king's word prevailed against Joab. Therefore,

Joab departed and went throughout all Israel, and came to Jerusalem. Joab gave the number of the census of all the people to David. And all Israel were 1,100,000 men who drew the sword; and Judah was 470,000 men who drew the sword. But he did not number Levi and Benjamin among them, for the king's command was abhorrent to Joab.

God was displeased with this thing, so He struck Israel.

David said to God, "I have sinned greatly, in that I have done this thing. But now, please take away the iniquity of Your servant, for I have done very foolishly."

The Lord spoke to Gad, David's seer, saying, "Go and speak to David, saying, 'Thus says the Lord, "I offer you three things; choose for yourself one of them, which I will do to you."'"

So Gad came to David and said to him, "Thus says the Lord, 'Take for yourself either three years of famine, or three months to be swept away before your foes, while the sword of your enemies overtakes you, or else three days of the sword of the Lord, even pestilence in the land, and the **angel** of the Lord destroying throughout all the territory of Israel.' Now, therefore, consider what answer I shall return to Him who sent me."

David said to Gad, "I am in great distress; please let me fall into the hand of the Lord, for His mercies are very great. But do not let me fall into the hand of man."

So the Lord sent a pestilence on Israel; 70,000 men of Israel fell.

And God sent an **angel** to Jerusalem to destroy it; but as he was about to destroy it, the Lord saw and was sorry over the calamity, and said to the destroying **angel**, "It is enough; now relax your hand." And the **angel** of the Lord was standing by the threshing floor of Ornan the Jebusite.

Then David lifted up his eyes and saw the **angel** of the Lord standing between earth and heaven, with his drawn sword in his hand stretched out over Jerusalem.

Then David and the elders, covered with sackcloth, fell on their faces. David said to God, "Is it not I who commanded to count the people? Indeed, I am the one who has sinned and done very wickedly, but these sheep, what have they done? O Lord my God, please let Your hand be against me and my father's household, but not against Your people that they should be plagued."

Then the **angel** of the Lord commanded Gad to say to David, that David should go up and build an altar to the Lord on the threshing floor of Ornan the Jebusite. So David went up at the word of Gad, which he spoke in the name of the Lord.

Now Ornan turned back and saw the **angel**, and his four sons who were with him hid themselves. And Ornan was threshing wheat.

1 Chronicles 21:1 - 22:2 > continued

As David came to Ornan, Ornan looked and saw David, and went out from the threshing floor and prostrated himself before David with his face to the ground.

Then David said to Ornan, "Give me the site of this threshing floor, that I may build on it an altar to the Lord; for the full price you shall give it to me, that the plague may be restrained from the people."

Ornan said to David, "Take it for yourself; and let my lord the king do what is good in his sight. See, I will give the oxen for burnt offerings and the threshing sledges for wood and the wheat for the grain offering; I will give it all."

But King David said to Ornan, "No, but I will surely buy it for the full price; for I will not take what is yours for the Lord, or offer a burnt offering which costs me nothing."

So David gave Ornan 600 shekels of gold by weight for the site. Then David built an altar to the Lord there and offered burnt offerings and peace offerings. And he called to the Lord and He answered him with fire from heaven on the altar of burnt offering.

The Lord commanded the **angel**, and he put his sword back in its sheath. At that time, when David saw that the Lord had answered him on the threshing floor of Ornan the Jebusite, he offered sacrifice there. For the tabernacle of the Lord, which Moses had made in the wilderness, and the altar of burnt offering were in the high place at Gibeon at that time. But David could not go before it to inquire of God, for he was terrified by the sword of the **angel** of the Lord.

Then David said, "This is the house of the Lord God, and this is the altar of burnt offering for Israel."

So David gave orders to gather the foreigners who were in the land of Israel, and he set stonecutters to hew out stones to build the house of God.

> 1 Chronicles 21:1 - 22:2

Sennacherib king of Assyria sent his servants to Jerusalem while he was besieging Lachish with all his forces with him, against Hezekiah king of Judah and against all Judah who were at Jerusalem, saying, "Thus says Sennacherib king of Assyria, 'On what are you trusting that you are remaining in Jerusalem under siege? Is not Hezekiah misleading you to give yourselves over to die by hunger and by thirst, saying, "The Lord our God will deliver us from the hand of the king of Assyria"?' " ...

... His servants spoke further against the Lord God and against His servant Hezekiah. He also wrote letters to insult the Lord God of Israel, and to speak against Him, saying, "As the gods of the nations of the lands have not delivered their people from my hand, so the God of Hezekiah will not deliver His people from my hand."

They called this out with a loud voice in the language of Judah to the people of Jerusalem who were on the wall, to frighten and terrify them, so that they might take the city.

They spoke of the God of Jerusalem as of the gods of the peoples of the earth, the work of men's hands. But King Hezekiah and Isaiah the prophet, the son of Amoz, prayed about this and cried out to heaven.

And the Lord sent an **angel** who destroyed every mighty warrior, commander and officer in the camp of the king of Assyria. So he returned in shame to his own land. And when he had entered the temple of his god, some of his own children killed him there with the sword.

So the Lord saved Hezekiah and the inhabitants of Jerusalem from the hand of Sennacherib the king of Assyria and from the hand of all others, and guided them on every side.   *2 Chronicles 32:9-11...16-22*

There was a day when the **sons of God** came to present themselves before the Lord, and Satan also came among them.   *Job 1:6*

Again there was a day when the **sons of God** came to present themselves before the Lord, and Satan also came among them to present himself before the Lord.   *Job 2:1*

Can mankind be just before God? Can a man be pure before his Maker? He puts no trust even in His servants; and against His **angels** He charges error. How much more those who dwell in houses of clay, whose foundation is in the dust, who are crushed before the moth!

Between morning and evening they are broken in pieces; unobserved, they perish forever. Is not their tent-cord plucked up within them? They die, yet without wisdom.

Call now, is there anyone who will answer you? And to which of the **holy ones** will you turn?   *Job 4:17 - 5:1*

What is man, that he should be pure, or he who is born of a woman, that he should be righteous?

Behold, He puts no trust in His **holy ones**, and the heavens are not pure in His sight; how much less one who is detestable and corrupt, man, who drinks iniquity like water!   *Job 15:14-16*

Man is also chastened with pain on his bed, and with unceasing complaint in his bones; so that his life loathes bread, and his soul favorite food. His flesh wastes away from sight, and his bones which were not seen stick out. Then his soul draws near to the pit, and his life to those who bring death.

If there is an **angel** as mediator for him, one out of a thousand, to
Job 33:19-26 > continued

remind a man what is right for him, then let him be gracious to him, and say, "Deliver him from going down to the pit, I have found a ransom"; let his flesh become fresher than in youth, let him return to the days of his youthful vigor; then he will pray to God, and He will accept him, that he may see His face with joy, and He may restore His righteousness to man.
> Job 33:19-26

The Lord answered Job out of the whirlwind and said, "Who is this that darkens counsel by words without knowledge? Now gird up your loins like a man, and I will ask you, and you instruct Me!

"Where were you when I laid the foundation of the earth? Tell Me, if you have understanding, who set its measurements? Since you know. Or who stretched the line on it? On what were its bases sunk? Or who laid its cornerstone, when the morning **stars** sang together and all the **sons of God** shouted for joy?"
Job 38:1-7

In my distress I called upon the Lord, and cried to my God for help; He heard my voice out of His temple, and my cry for help before Him came into His ears.

Then the earth shook and quaked; and the foundations of the mountains were trembling and were shaken, because He was angry. Smoke went up out of His nostrils, and fire from His mouth devoured; coals were kindled by it.

He bowed the heavens also, and came down With thick darkness under His feet. He rode upon a **cherub** and flew; and He sped upon the wings of the wind.

He made darkness His hiding place, His canopy around Him, darkness of waters, thick clouds of the skies.
Psalm 18:6-11

I sought the Lord, and He answered me, and delivered me from all my fears. They looked to Him and were radiant, and their faces will never be ashamed. This poor man cried, and the Lord heard him and saved him out of all his troubles.

The **angel** of the Lord encamps around those who fear Him, and rescues them. O taste and see that the Lord is good; how blessed is the man who takes refuge in Him!
Psalm 34:4-8

Let those be ashamed and dishonored who seek my life; let those be turned back and humiliated who devise evil against me. Let them be like chaff before the wind, with the **angel** of the Lord driving them on.

Let their way be dark and slippery, with the **angel** of the Lord pursuing them. For without cause they hid their net for me; without cause they dug a pit for my soul.

Let destruction come upon him unawares, and let the net which he hid catch himself; into that very destruction let him fall. And my soul shall rejoice in the Lord; it shall exult in His salvation. *Psalm 35:4-9*

They spoke against God; they said, "Can God prepare a table in the wilderness? Behold, He struck the rock so that waters gushed out, and streams were overflowing; can He give bread also? Will He provide meat for His people?"

Therefore the Lord heard and was full of wrath; and a fire was kindled against Jacob and anger also mounted against Israel, because they did not believe in God and did not trust in His salvation.

Yet He commanded the clouds above and opened the doors of heaven; He rained down manna upon them to eat and gave them food from heaven. Man did eat the bread of **angels**; He sent them food in abundance. *Psalm 78:19-25*

He gave also their crops to the grasshopper and the product of their labor to the locust. He destroyed their vines with hailstones and their sycamore trees with frost. He gave over their cattle also to the hailstones and their herds to bolts of lightning.

He sent upon them His burning anger, fury and indignation and trouble, a band of destroying **angels**. He leveled a path for His anger; he did not spare their soul from death, but gave over their life to the plague, and smote all the firstborn in Egypt, the first issue of their virility in the tents of Ham. *Psalm 78:46-51*

The heavens will praise Your wonders, O Lord; Your faithfulness also in the assembly of the **holy ones**. For who in the skies is comparable to the Lord? Who among the sons of the mighty is like the Lord, a God greatly feared in the council of the **holy ones**, and awesome above all those who are around Him? O Lord God of hosts, who is like You, O mighty Lord? Your faithfulness also surrounds You. *Psalm 89:5-8*

You have made the Lord, my refuge, even the Most High, your dwelling place. No evil will befall you, nor will any plague come near your tent. For He will give His **angels** charge concerning you, to guard you in all your ways.

They will bear you up in their hands, that you do not strike your foot against a stone. You will tread upon the lion and cobra, the young lion and the serpent you will trample down. *Psalm 91:9-13*

The Lord has established His throne in the heavens, and His sovereignty rules over all. Bless the Lord, you His **angels**, mighty in strength, who perform His word, obeying the voice of His word!

Bless the Lord, all you His hosts, you who serve Him, doing His will. Bless the Lord, all you works of His, in all places of His dominion; bless the Lord, O my soul! *Psalm 103:19-22*

Praise the Lord! Praise the Lord from the heavens; praise Him in the heights! Praise Him, all His **angels**; praise Him, all His hosts! Praise Him, sun and moon; praise Him, all stars of light! Praise Him, highest heavens, and the waters that are above the heavens!

Let them praise the name of the Lord, for He commanded and they were created. He has also established them forever and ever; He has made a decree which will not pass away. *Psalm 148:1-6*

In the year of King Uzziah's death I saw the Lord sitting on a throne, lofty and exalted, with the train of His robe filling the temple.

Seraphim stood above Him, each having six wings: with two he covered his face, and with two he covered his feet, and with two he flew. And one called out to another and said, "Holy, Holy, Holy, is the Lord of hosts, the whole earth is full of His glory."

And the foundations of the thresholds trembled at the voice of him who called out, while the temple was filling with smoke.

Then I said, "Woe is me, for I am ruined! Because I am a man of unclean lips, and I live among a people of unclean lips; for my eyes have seen the King, the Lord of hosts."

Then one of the **seraphim** flew to me with a burning coal in his hand, which he had taken from the altar with tongs.

He touched my mouth with it and said, "Behold, this has touched your lips; and your iniquity is taken away and your sin is forgiven."

Isaiah 6:1-7

Thus says the Lord concerning the king of Assyria, "He will not come to this city or shoot an arrow there; and he will not come before it with a shield, or throw up a siege ramp against it. By the way that he came, by the same he will return, and he will not come to this city," declares the Lord, "for I will defend this city to save it for My own sake and for My servant David's sake."

Then the **angel** of the Lord went out and struck 185,000 in the camp of the Assyrians; and when men arose early in the morning, behold, all of these were dead.

So Sennacherib king of Assyria departed and returned home and lived at Nineveh. *Isaiah 37:33-37*

I shall make mention of the lovingkindnesses of the Lord, the praises of the Lord, according to all that the Lord has granted us, and the great goodness toward the house of Israel, which He has granted them according to His compassion and according to the abundance of His lovingkindnesses.

For He said, "Surely, they are My people, sons who will not deal falsely." So He became their Savior. In all their affliction He was afflicted, and the **angel** of His presence saved them; in His love and in His mercy He redeemed them, and He lifted them and carried them all the days of old.   *Isaiah 63:7-9*

As I looked, behold, a storm wind was coming from the north, a great cloud with fire flashing forth continually and a bright light around it, and in its midst something like glowing metal in the midst of the fire. Within it there were figures resembling four living beings.

And this was their appearance: they had human form. Each of them had four faces and four wings. Their legs were straight and their feet were like a calf's hoof, and they gleamed like burnished bronze. Under their wings on their four sides were human hands.

As for the faces and wings of the four of them, their wings touched one another; their faces did not turn when they moved, each went straight forward.

As for the form of their faces, each had the face of a man; all four had the face of a lion on the right and the face of a bull on the left, and all four had the face of an eagle. Such were their faces.

Their wings were spread out above; each had two touching another being, and two covering their bodies. And each went straight forward; wherever the spirit was about to go, they would go, without turning as they went.

In the midst of the living beings there was something that looked like burning coals of fire, like torches darting back and forth among the living beings. The fire was bright, and lightning was flashing from the fire. And the living beings ran to and fro like bolts of lightning.

Now as I looked at the living beings, behold, there was one wheel on the earth beside the living beings, for each of the four of them. The appearance of the wheels and their workmanship was like sparkling beryl, and all four of them had the same form, their appearance and workmanship being as if one wheel were within another.

Whenever they moved, they moved in any of their four directions without turning as they moved. As for their rims they were lofty and awesome, and the rims of all four of them were full of eyes round about.

Whenever the living beings moved, the wheels moved with them. And whenever the living beings rose from the earth, the wheels rose also. Wherever the spirit was about to go, they would go in that direction. And the wheels rose close beside them; for the spirit of the living beings was in the wheels.

Whenever those went, these

Ezekiel 1:4-25 > continued

went; and whenever those stood still, these stood still. And whenever those rose from the earth, the wheels rose close beside them; for the spirit of the living beings was in the wheels.

Now over the heads of the living beings there was something like an expanse, like the awesome gleam of crystal, spread out over their heads. Under the expanse their wings were stretched out straight, one toward the other; each one also had two wings covering its body on the one side and on the other.

I also heard the sound of their wings like the sound of abundant waters as they went, like the voice of the Almighty, a sound of tumult like the sound of an army camp; whenever they stood still, they dropped their wings.

And there came a voice from above the expanse that was over their heads; whenever they stood still, they dropped their wings.

> *Ezekiel 1:4-25*

It came about in the sixth year, on the fifth day of the sixth month, as I was sitting in my house with the elders of Judah sitting before me, that the hand of the Lord God fell on me there.

Then I looked, and behold, a likeness as the appearance of a man; from His loins and downward there was the appearance of fire, and from His loins and upward the appearance of brightness, like the appearance of glowing metal.

He stretched out the form of a hand and caught me by a lock of my head; and the Spirit lifted me up between earth and heaven and brought me in the visions of God to Jerusalem, to the entrance of the north gate of the inner court, where the seat of the idol of jealousy, which provokes to jealousy, was located.

And behold, the glory of the God of Israel was there, like the appearance which I saw in the plain.

Then He said to me, "Son of man, raise your eyes now toward the north." So I raised my eyes toward the north, and behold, to the north of the altar gate was this idol of jealousy at the entrance.

And He said to me, "Son of man, do you see what they are doing, the great abominations which the house of Israel are committing here, so that I would be far from My sanctuary? But yet you will see still greater abominations."   *Ezekiel 8:1-6*

Behold, six men came from the direction of the upper gate which faces north, each with his shattering weapon in his hand; and among them was a certain man clothed in linen with a writing case at his loins. And they went in and stood beside the bronze altar.

Then the glory of the God of Israel went up from the **cherub** on which it had been, to the threshold of the temple. And He called to the man clothed in linen at whose loins was the writing case.

The Lord said to him, "Go through the midst of the city, even through the midst of Jerusalem, and put a mark on the foreheads of the men who sigh and groan over all the abominations which are being committed in its midst."

But to the others He said in my hearing, "Go through the city after him and strike; do not let your eye have pity and do not spare. Utterly slay old men, young men, maidens, little children, and women, but do not touch any man on whom is the mark; and you shall start from My sanctuary."

So they started with the elders who were before the temple.

And He said to them, "Defile the temple and fill the courts with the slain. Go out!"

Thus they went out and struck down the people in the city.

Ezekiel 9:2-7

Then I looked, and behold, in the expanse that was over the heads of the **cherubim** something like a sapphire stone, in appearance resembling a throne, appeared above them.

He spoke to the man clothed in linen and said, "Enter between the whirling wheels under the **cherubim** and fill your hands with coals of fire from between the **cherubim** and scatter them over the city." And he entered in my sight.

Now the **cherubim** were standing on the right side of the temple when the man entered, and the cloud filled the inner court.

Then the glory of the Lord went up from the **cherub** to the threshold of the temple, and the temple was filled with the cloud and the court was filled with the brightness of the glory of the Lord. Moreover, the sound of the wings of the **cherubim** was heard as far as the outer court, like the voice of God Almighty when He speaks.

It came about when He commanded the man clothed in linen, saying, "Take fire from between the whirling wheels, from between the **cherubim**," he entered and stood beside a wheel.

Then the **cherub** stretched out his hand from between the **cherubim** to the fire which was between the **cherubim**, took some and put it into the hands of the one clothed in linen, who took it and went out. The **cherubim** appeared to have the form of a man's hand under their wings.

Then I looked, and behold, four wheels beside the **cherubim**, one wheel beside each **cherub**; and the appearance of the wheels was like the gleam of a Tarshish stone. As for their appearance, all four of them had the same likeness, as if one wheel were within another wheel.

When they moved, they went in any of their four directions without

Ezekiel 10:1-22 > continued

turning as they went; but they followed in the direction which they faced, without turning as they went. Their whole body, their backs, their hands, their wings and the wheels were full of eyes all around, the wheels belonging to all four of them. The wheels were called in my hearing, the whirling wheels.

And each one had four faces. The first face was the face of a **cherub**, the second face was the face of a man, the third the face of a lion, and the fourth the face of an eagle.

Then the **cherubim** rose up. They are the living beings that I saw by the river Chebar.

Now when the **cherubim** moved, the wheels would go beside them; also when the **cherubim** lifted up their wings to rise from the ground, the wheels would not turn from beside them.

When the **cherubim** stood still, the wheels would stand still; and when they rose up, the wheels would rise with them, for the spirit of the living beings was in them.

Then the glory of the Lord departed from the threshold of the temple and stood over the **cherubim**.

When the **cherubim** departed, they lifted their wings and rose up from the earth in my sight with the wheels beside them; and they stood still at the entrance of the east gate of the Lord's house, and the glory of the God of Israel hovered over them. These are the living beings that I saw beneath the God of Israel by the river Chebar; so I knew that they were **cherubim**.

Each one had four faces and each one four wings, and beneath their wings was the form of human hands. As for the likeness of their faces, they were the same faces whose appearance I had seen by the river Chebar. Each one went straight ahead. *> Ezekiel 10:1-22*

The **cherubim** lifted up their wings with the wheels beside them, and the glory of the God of Israel hovered over them.

The glory of the Lord went up from the midst of the city and stood over the mountain which is east of the city. *Ezekiel 11:22-23*

Nebuchadnezzar the king was astounded and stood up in haste; he said to his high officials, "Was it not three men we cast bound into the midst of the fire?"

They replied to the king, "Certainly, O king."

He said, "Look! I see four men loosed and walking about in the midst of the fire without harm, and the appearance of the fourth is like a son of the gods!"

Then Nebuchadnezzar came near to the door of the furnace of blazing fire; he responded and said, "Shadrach, Meshach and Abednego, come out, you servants of the Most High God, and come here!"

Then Shadrach, Meshach and Abednego came out of the midst of the fire.

The satraps, the prefects, the governors and the king's high officials gathered around and saw in regard to these men that the fire had
no effect on the bodies of these men nor was the hair of their head
singed, nor were their trousers damaged, nor had the smell of fire even
come upon them.

Nebuchadnezzar responded and said, "Blessed be the God of
Shadrach, Meshach and Abednego, who has sent His **angel** and delivered His servants who put their trust in Him, violating the king's command, and yielded up their bodies so as not to serve or worship any
god except their own God."   *Daniel 3:24-28*

I was looking in the visions in my mind as I lay on my bed, and behold,
an **angelic** watcher, a **holy one**, descended from heaven.

He shouted out and spoke as follows: "Chop down the tree and cut
off its branches, strip off its foliage and scatter its fruit; let the beasts
flee from under it and the birds from its branches. Yet leave the stump
with its roots in the ground, but with a band of iron and bronze around it
in the new grass of the field; and let him be drenched with the dew of
heaven, and let him share with the beasts in the grass of the earth.

"Let his mind be changed from that of a man and let a beast's mind
be given to him, and let seven periods of time pass over him.

"This sentence is by the decree of the **angelic** watchers and the
decision is a command of the **holy ones**, in order that the living may
know that the Most High is ruler over the realm of mankind, and bestows it on whom He wishes and sets over it the lowliest of men.

"This is the dream which I, King Nebuchadnezzar, have seen.
Now you, Belteshazzar, tell me its interpretation, inasmuch as none of
the wise men of my kingdom is able to make known to me the interpretation; but you are able, for a spirit of the holy gods is in you."

Then Daniel, whose name is Belteshazzar, was appalled for a
while as his thoughts alarmed him.

The king responded and said, Belteshazzar, do not let the dream
or its interpretation alarm you."

Belteshazzar replied, "My lord, if only the dream applied to those
who hate you and its interpretation to your adversaries! The tree that
you saw, which became large and grew strong, whose height reached
to the sky and was visible to all the earth and whose foliage was beautiful and its fruit abundant, and in which was food for all, under which
the beasts of the field dwelt and in whose branches the birds of the sky
lodged - it is you, O king; for you have become great and grown strong,
and your majesty has become great and reached to the sky and your
dominion to the end of the earth.

Daniel 4:13-25 > continued

"In that the king saw an **angelic** watcher, a **holy one**, descending from heaven and saying, 'Chop down the tree and destroy it; yet leave the stump with its roots in the ground, but with a band of iron and bronze around it in the new grass of the field, and let him be drenched with the dew of heaven, and let him share with the beasts of the field until seven periods of time pass over him,' this is the interpretation, O king, and this is the decree of the Most High, which has come upon my lord the king: that you be driven away from mankind and your dwelling place be with the beasts of the field, and you be given grass to eat like cattle and be drenched with the dew of heaven; and seven periods of time will pass over you, until you recognize that the Most High is ruler over the realm of mankind and bestows it on whomever He wishes."

> *Daniel 4:13-25*

The king gave orders, and Daniel was brought in and cast into the lions' den.

The king spoke and said to Daniel, "Your God whom you constantly serve will Himself deliver you."

A stone was brought and laid over the mouth of the den; and the king sealed it with his own signet ring and with the signet rings of his nobles, so that nothing would be changed in regard to Daniel.

Then the king went off to his palace and spent the night fasting, and no entertainment was brought before him; and his sleep fled from him.

Then the king arose at dawn, at the break of day, and went in haste to the lions' den. When he had come near the den to Daniel, he cried out with a troubled voice.

The king spoke and said to Daniel, "Daniel, servant of the living God, has your God, whom you constantly serve, been able to deliver you from the lions?"

Then Daniel spoke to the king, "O king, live forever! My God sent His **angel** and shut the lions' mouths and they have not harmed me, inasmuch as I was found innocent before Him; and also toward you, O king, I have committed no crime."

Then the king was very pleased and gave orders for Daniel to be taken up out of the den.

So Daniel was taken up out of the den and no injury whatever was found on him, because he had trusted in his God. *Daniel 6:16-23*

I heard a **holy one** speaking, and another **holy one** said to that particular one who was speaking, "How long will the vision about the regular sacrifice apply, while the transgression causes horror, so as to allow both the holy place and the host to be trampled?"

He said to me, "For 2,300 evenings and mornings; then the holy place will be properly restored."

When I, Daniel, had seen the vision, I sought to understand it; and behold, standing before me was one who looked like a man.

And I heard the voice of a man between the banks of Ulai, and he called out and said, "Gabriel, give this man an understanding of the vision."

So he came near to where I was standing, and when he came I was frightened and fell on my face; but he said to me, "Son of man, understand that the vision pertains to the time of the end."

Now while he was talking with me, I sank into a deep sleep with my face to the ground; but he touched me and made me stand upright.

He said, "Behold, I am going to let you know what will occur at the final period of the indignation, for it pertains to the appointed time of the end.

"The ram which you saw with the two horns represents the kings of Media and Persia. The shaggy goat represents the kingdom of Greece, and the large horn that is between his eyes is the first king. The broken horn and the four horns that arose in its place represent four kingdoms which will arise from his nation, although not with his power.

"In the latter period of their rule, when the transgressors have run their course, a king will arise, insolent and skilled in intrigue. His power will be mighty, but not by his own power, and he will destroy to an extraordinary degree and prosper and perform his will; he will destroy mighty men and the holy people.

"And through his shrewdness he will cause deceit to succeed by his influence; and he will magnify himself in his heart, and he will destroy many while they are at ease. He will even oppose the Prince of princes, but he will be broken without human agency.

"The vision of the evenings and mornings which has been told is true; but keep the vision secret, for it pertains to many days in the future."

Daniel 8:13-26

I, Daniel, looked and behold, two others were standing, one on this bank of the river and the other on that bank of the river.

And one said to the man dressed in linen, who was above the waters of the river, "How long will it be until the end of these wonders?"

I heard the man dressed in linen, who was above the waters of the river, as he raised his right hand and his left toward heaven, and swore by Him who lives forever that it would be for a time, times, and half a time; and as soon as they finish shattering the power of the holy people, all these events will be completed.

As for me, I heard but could not understand; so I said, "My lord, what will be the outcome of these events?"   *Daniel 12:5-10 > continued*

He said, "Go your way, Daniel, for these words are concealed and sealed up until the end time. Many will be purged, purified and refined, but the wicked will act wickedly; and none of the wicked will understand, but those who have insight will understand." *> Daniel 12:5-10*

Ephraim feeds on wind, and pursues the east wind continually; he multiplies lies and violence. Moreover, he makes a covenant with Assyria, and oil is carried to Egypt.

The Lord also has a dispute with Judah, and will punish Jacob according to his ways; He will repay him according to his deeds. In the womb he took his brother by the heel, and in his maturity he contended with God. Yes, he wrestled with the **angel** and prevailed; he wept and sought His favor.

He found Him at Bethel and there He spoke with us, even the Lord, the God of hosts, the Lord is His name.

Therefore, return to your God, observe kindness and justice, and wait for your God continually. *Hosea 12:1-6*

On the twenty-fourth day of the eleventh month, which is the month Shebat, in the second year of Darius, the word of the Lord came to Zechariah the prophet, the son of Berechiah, the son of Iddo, as follows: I saw at night, and behold, a man was riding on a red horse, and he was standing among the myrtle trees which were in the ravine, with red, sorrel and white horses behind him.

Then I said, "My lord, what are these?"

And the **angel** who was speaking with me said to me, "I will show you what these are."

And the man who was standing among the myrtle trees answered and said, "These are those whom the Lord has sent to patrol the earth."

So they answered the **angel** of the Lord who was standing among the myrtle trees and said, "We have patrolled the earth, and behold, all the earth is peaceful and quiet."

Then the **angel** of the Lord said, "O Lord of hosts, how long will You have no compassion for Jerusalem and the cities of Judah, with which You have been indignant these seventy years?"

The Lord answered the **angel** who was speaking with me with gracious words, comforting words.

So the **angel** who was speaking with me said to me, "Proclaim, saying, 'Thus says the Lord of hosts, "I am exceedingly jealous for Jerusalem and Zion. But I am very angry with the nations who are at ease; for while I was only a little angry, they furthered the disaster.

"Therefore thus says the Lord, 'I will return to Jerusalem with compassion; My house will be built in it,' declares the Lord of hosts, 'and a measuring line will be stretched over Jerusalem.'

"Again, proclaim, saying, 'Thus says the Lord of hosts, "My cities will again overflow with prosperity, and the Lord will again comfort Zion and again choose Jerusalem."'"

Then I lifted up my eyes and looked, and behold, there were four horns. So I said to the **angel** who was speaking with me, "What are these?"

And he answered me, "These are the horns which have scattered Judah, Israel and Jerusalem."

Then the Lord showed me four craftsmen. I said, "What are these coming to do?"

And he said, "These are the horns which have scattered Judah so that no man lifts up his head; but these craftsmen have come to terrify them, to throw down the horns of the nations who have lifted up their horns against the land of Judah in order to scatter it."

Then I lifted up my eyes and looked, and behold, there was a man with a measuring line in his hand. So I said, "Where are you going?"

And he said to me, "To measure Jerusalem, to see how wide it is and how long it is."

And behold, the **angel** who was speaking with me was going out, and another **angel** was coming out to meet him, and said to him, "Run, speak to that young man, saying, 'Jerusalem will be inhabited without walls because of the multitude of men and cattle within it. For I,' declares the Lord, 'will be a wall of fire around her, and I will be the glory in her midst.' " *Zechariah 1:7 - 2:5*

He showed me Joshua, the high priest, standing before the **angel** of the Lord, and Satan standing at his right hand to accuse him.

The Lord said to Satan, "The Lord rebuke you, Satan! Indeed, the Lord who has chosen Jerusalem rebuke you! Is this not a brand plucked from the fire?"

Now Joshua was clothed with filthy garments and standing before the **angel**. He spoke and said to those who were standing before him, saying, "Remove the filthy garments from him."

Again he said to him, "See, I have taken your iniquity away from you and will clothe you with festal robes."

Then I said, "Let them put a clean turban on his head." So they put a clean turban on his head and clothed him with garments, while the **angel** of the Lord was standing by.

And the **angel** of the Lord admonished Joshua, saying, "Thus says the Lord of hosts, 'If you will walk in My ways and if you will perform My service, then you will also govern My house and also have charge of My courts, and I will grant you free access among these who are standing here.' " *Zechariah 3:1-7*

The **angel** who was speaking with me returned and roused me, as a man who is awakened from his sleep. He said to me, "What do you see?"

And I said, "I see, and behold, a lampstand all of gold with its bowl on the top of it, and its seven lamps on it with seven spouts belonging to each of the lamps which are on the top of it; also two olive trees by it, one on the right side of the bowl and the other on its left side."

Then I said to the **angel** who was speaking with me saying, "What are these, my lord?"

So the **angel** who was speaking with me answered and said to me, "Do you not know what these are?" And I said, "No, my lord."

Then he said to me, "This is the word of the Lord to Zerubbabel saying, 'Not by might nor by power, but by My Spirit,' says the Lord of hosts. 'What are you, O great mountain? Before Zerubbabel you will become a plain; and he will bring forth the top stone with shouts of "Grace, grace to it!"'"

Zechariah 4:1-7

The **angel** who was speaking with me went out and said to me, "Lift up now your eyes and see what this is going forth."

I said, "What is it?"

And he said, "This is the ephah going forth."

Again he said, "This is their appearance in all the land (and behold, a lead cover was lifted up); and this is a woman sitting inside the ephah."

Then he said, "This is Wickedness!" And he threw her down into the middle of the ephah and cast the lead weight on its opening.

Then I lifted up my eyes and looked, and there two women were coming out with the wind in their wings; and they had wings like the wings of a stork, and they lifted up the ephah between the earth and the heavens.

I said to the **angel** who was speaking with me, "Where are they taking the ephah?"

Then he said to me, "To build a temple for her in the land of Shinar; and when it is prepared, she will be set there on her own pedestal."

Now I lifted up my eyes again and looked, and behold, four chariots were coming forth from between the two mountains; and the mountains were bronze mountains. With the first chariot were red horses, with the second chariot black horses, with the third chariot white horses, and with the fourth chariot strong dappled horses.

Then I spoke and said to the **angel** who was speaking with me, "What are these, my lord?"

The **angel** replied to me, "These are the four spirits of heaven, going forth after standing before the Lord of all the earth, with one of which the black horses are going forth to the north country; and the white ones go forth after them, while the dappled ones go forth to the south country. When the strong ones went out, they were eager to go to patrol the earth."

And He said, "Go, patrol the earth." So they patrolled the earth.

Then He cried out to me and spoke to me saying, "See, those who are going to the land of the north have appeased My wrath in the land of the north." *Zechariah 5:5 - 6:8*

The Lord also will save the tents of Judah first, so that the glory of the house of David and the glory of the inhabitants of Jerusalem will not be magnified above Judah.

In that day the Lord will defend the inhabitants of Jerusalem, and the one who is feeble among them in that day will be like David, and the house of David will be like God, like the **angel** of the Lord before them.

And in that day I will set about to destroy all the nations that come against Jerusalem. I will pour out on the house of David and on the inhabitants of Jerusalem, the Spirit of grace and of supplication, so that they will look on Me whom they have pierced; and they will mourn for Him, as one mourns for an only son, and they will weep bitterly over Him like the bitter weeping over a firstborn. *Zechariah 12:7-9*

Then the Lord will go forth and fight against those nations, as when He fights on a day of battle. In that day His feet will stand on the Mount of Olives, which is in front of Jerusalem on the east; and the Mount of Olives will be split in its middle from east to west by a very large valley, so that half of the mountain will move toward the north and the other half toward the south.

You will flee by the valley of My mountains, for the valley of the mountains will reach to Azel; yes, you will flee just as you fled before the earthquake in the days of Uzziah king of Judah.

Then the Lord, my God, will come, and all the **holy ones** with Him! *Zechariah 14:3-5*

~ End of Old Testament Scriptures ~

NEW TESTAMENT

The birth of Jesus Christ was as follows: when His mother Mary had been betrothed to Joseph, before they came together she was found to be with child by the Holy Spirit.

And Joseph her husband, being a righteous man and not wanting to disgrace her, planned to send her away secretly.

But when he had considered this, behold, an **angel** of the Lord appeared to him in a dream, saying, "Joseph, son of David, do not be afraid to take Mary as your wife; for the Child who has been conceived in her is of the Holy Spirit.

"She will bear a Son; and you shall call His name Jesus, for He will save His people from their sins."

Now all this took place to fulfill what was spoken by the Lord through the prophet: "Behold, the virgin shall be with child and shall bear a Son, and they shall call His name Immanuel," which translated means, "God with us."

And Joseph awoke from his sleep and did as the **angel** of the Lord commanded him, and took Mary as his wife, but kept her a virgin until she gave birth to a Son; and he called His name Jesus.   *Matthew 1:18-25*

When they had gone, behold, an **angel** of the Lord appeared to Joseph in a dream and said, "Get up! Take the Child and His mother and flee to Egypt, and remain there until I tell you; for Herod is going to search for the Child to destroy Him."

So Joseph got up and took the Child and His mother while it was still night, and left for Egypt.

He remained there until the death of Herod. This was to fulfill what had been spoken by the Lord through the prophet: "Out of Egypt I called My Son."   *Matthew 2:13-15*

When Herod died, behold, an **angel** of the Lord appeared in a dream to Joseph in Egypt, and said, "Get up, take the Child and His mother, and go into the land of Israel; for those who sought the Child's life are dead."

So Joseph got up, took the Child and His mother, and came into the land of Israel.   *Matthew 2:19-21*

The devil took Him into the holy city and had Him stand on the pinnacle of the temple, and said to Him, "If You are the Son of God, throw Yourself down; for it is written, 'He will command His **angels** concerning You'; and 'On their hands they will bear You up, so that You will not strike Your foot against a stone.' "

Jesus said to him, "On the other hand, it is written, 'You shall not put the Lord your God to the test.' "

Again, the devil took Him to a very high mountain and showed Him all the kingdoms of the world and their glory; and he said to Him, "All these things I will give You, if You fall down and worship me."

Then Jesus said to him, "Go, Satan! For it is written, 'You shall worship the Lord your God, and serve Him only' "

Then the devil left Him; and behold, **angels** came and began to minister to Him.   *Matthew 4:5-11*

Blessed are the merciful, for they shall receive mercy. Blessed are the pure in heart, for they shall see God.

Blessed are the peacemakers, for they shall be called **sons of God**.

Blessed are those who have been persecuted for the sake of right-eousness, for theirs is the kingdom of heaven.   *Matthew 5:8-10*

All these things Jesus spoke to the crowds in parables, and He did not speak to them without a parable. This was to fulfill what was spoken through the prophet: "I will open My mouth in parables; I will utter things hidden since the foundation of the world." Then He left the crowds and went into the house.

And His disciples came to Him and said, "Explain to us the parable of the tares of the field."

And He said, "The one who sows the good seed is the Son of Man, and the field is the world; and as for the good seed, these are the sons of the kingdom; and the tares are the sons of the evil one; and the enemy who sowed them is the devil, and the harvest is the end of the age; and the reapers are **angels**.

"So just as the tares are gathered up and burned with fire, so shall it be at the end of the age. The Son of Man will send forth His **angels**, and they will gather out of His kingdom all stumbling blocks, and those who commit lawlessness, and will throw them into the furnace of fire; in that place there will be weeping and gnashing of teeth.

"Then the righteous will shine forth as the sun in the kingdom of their Father. He who has ears, let him hear."   *Matthew 13:34-43*

The kingdom of heaven is like a dragnet cast into the sea, and gather-ing fish of every kind; and when it was filled, they drew it up on the beach; and they sat down and gathered the good fish into containers, but the bad they threw away.

So it will be at the end of the age; the **angels** will come forth and take out the wicked from among the righteous, and will throw them into the furnace of fire; in that place there will be weeping and gnashing of teeth.   *Matthew 13:47-50*

Jesus said to His disciples, "If anyone wishes to come after Me, he must deny himself, and take up his cross and follow Me. For whoever wishes to save his life will lose it; but whoever loses his life for My sake will find it.

"For what will it profit a man if he gains the whole world and forfeits his soul? Or what will a man give in exchange for his soul?

"For the Son of Man is going to come in the glory of His Father with His **angels**, and will then repay every man according to his deeds."   *Matthew 16:24-27*

See that you do not despise one of these little ones, for I say to you that their **angels** in heaven continually see the face of My Father who is in heaven.   *Matthew 18:10*

On that day some Sadducees (who say there is no resurrection) came to Jesus and questioned Him, asking, "Teacher, Moses said, 'If a man dies having no children, his brother as next of kin shall marry his wife, and raise up children for his brother.'

"Now there were seven brothers with us; and the first married and died, and having no children left his wife to his brother; so also the second, and the third, down to the seventh. Last of all, the woman died. In the resurrection, therefore, whose wife of the seven will she be? For they all had married her."

But Jesus answered and said to them, "You are mistaken, not understanding the Scriptures nor the power of God. For in the resurrection they neither marry nor are given in marriage, but are like **angels** in heaven."   *Matthew 22:23-30*

Immediately after the tribulation of those days the sun will be darkened, and the moon will not give its light, and the stars will fall from the sky, and the powers of the heavens will be shaken.

And then the sign of the Son of Man will appear in the sky, and then all the tribes of the earth will mourn, and they will see the Son of Man coming on the clouds of the sky with power and great glory.

And He will send forth His **angels** with a great trumpet and they will gather together His elect from the four winds, from one end of the sky to the other.   *Matthew 24:29-31*

Truly I say to you, this generation will not pass away until all these things take place. Heaven and earth will pass away, but My words will not pass away.

But of that day and hour no one knows, not even the **angels** of heaven, nor the Son, but the Father alone.   *Matthew 24:34-36*

When the Son of Man comes in His glory, and all the **angels** with Him, then He will sit on His glorious throne. All the nations will be gathered before Him; and He will separate them from one another, as the shepherd separates the sheep from the goats; and He will put the sheep on His right, and the goats on the left.

Then the King will say to those on His right, "Come, you who are blessed of My Father, inherit the kingdom prepared for you from the foundation of the world. For I was hungry, and you gave Me something to eat; I was thirsty, and you gave Me something to drink; I was a stranger, and you invited Me in; naked, and you clothed Me; I was sick, and you visited Me; I was in prison, and you came to Me." ...

... Then He will also say to those on His left, "Depart from Me, accursed ones, into the eternal fire which has been prepared for the devil and his **angels**; for I was hungry, and you gave Me nothing to eat; I was thirsty, and you gave Me nothing to drink; I was a stranger, and you did not invite Me in; naked, and you did not clothe Me; sick, and in prison, and you did not visit Me."   *Matthew 25:31-36...41-43*

Jesus said to him, "Friend, do what you have come for."

Then they came and laid hands on Jesus and seized Him. And behold, one of those who were with Jesus reached and drew out his sword, and struck the slave of the high priest and cut off his ear.

Then Jesus said to him, "Put your sword back into its place; for all those who take up the sword shall perish by the sword. Or do you think that I cannot appeal to My Father, and He will at once put at My disposal more than twelve legions of **angels**?

"How then will the Scriptures be fulfilled, which say that it must happen this way?"   *Matthew 26:50-54*

After the Sabbath, as it began to dawn toward the first day of the week, Mary Magdalene and the other Mary came to look at the grave.

And behold, a severe earthquake had occurred, for an **angel** of the Lord descended from heaven and came and rolled away the stone and sat upon it. And his appearance was like lightning, and his clothing as white as snow.

The guards shook for fear of him and became like dead men.

The **angel** said to the women, "Do not be afraid; for I know that you are looking for Jesus who has been crucified. He is not here, for He has risen, just as He said. Come, see the place where He was lying.

"Go quickly and tell His disciples that He has risen from the dead; and behold, He is going ahead of you into Galilee, there you will see Him; behold, I have told you."   *Matthew 28:1-8 > continued*

And they left the tomb quickly with fear and great joy and ran to report it to His disciples.   *> Matthew 28:1-8*

In those days Jesus came from Nazareth in Galilee and was baptized by John in the Jordan.

Immediately coming up out of the water, He saw the heavens opening, and the Spirit like a dove descending upon Him; and a voice came out of the heavens: "You are My beloved Son, in You I am well-pleased."

Immediately the Spirit impelled Him to go out into the wilderness. And He was in the wilderness forty days being tempted by Satan; and He was with the wild beasts, and the **angels** were ministering to Him.
Mark 1:9-13

[Jesus] summoned the crowd with His disciples, and said to them, "If anyone wishes to come after Me, he must deny himself, and take up his cross and follow Me. For whoever wishes to save his life will lose it, but whoever loses his life for My sake and the gospel's will save it.

"For what does it profit a man to gain the whole world, and forfeit his soul? For what will a man give in exchange for his soul?

"For whoever is ashamed of Me and My words in this adulterous and sinful generation, the Son of Man will also be ashamed of him when He comes in the glory of His Father with the holy **angels**."
Mark 8:34-38

Some Sadducees (who say that there is no resurrection) came to Jesus, and began questioning Him, saying, "Teacher, Moses wrote for us that if a man's brother dies and leaves behind a wife and leaves no child, his brother should marry the wife and raise up children to his brother.

"There were seven brothers; and the first took a wife, and died leaving no children. The second one married her, and died leaving behind no children; and the third likewise; and so all seven left no children. Last of all the woman died also.

"In the resurrection, when they rise again, which one's wife will she be? For all seven had married her."

Jesus said to them, "Is this not the reason you are mistaken, that you do not understand the Scriptures or the power of God? For when they rise from the dead, they neither marry nor are given in marriage, but are like **angels** in heaven."   *Mark 12:18-25*

In those days, after that tribulation, the sun will be darkened and the moon will not give its light, and the stars will be falling from heaven, and the powers that are in the heavens will be shaken. Then they will see the Son of Man coming in clouds with great power and glory.

And then He will send forth the **angels**, and will gather together His elect from the four winds, from the farthest end of the earth to the farthest end of heaven. *Mark 13:24-27*

Of that day or hour no one knows, not even the **angels** in heaven, nor the Son, but the Father alone.

Take heed, keep on the alert; for you do not know when the appointed time will come. *Mark 13:32-33*

When the Sabbath was over, Mary Magdalene, and Mary the mother of James, and Salome, bought spices, so that they might come and anoint Him. Very early on the first day of the week, they came to the tomb when the sun had risen.

They were saying to one another, "Who will roll away the stone for us from the entrance of the tomb?"

Looking up, they saw that the stone had been rolled away, although it was extremely large.

Entering the tomb, they saw a young man sitting at the right, wearing a white robe; and they were amazed.

And he said to them, "Do not be amazed; you are looking for Jesus the Nazarene, who has been crucified. He has risen; He is not here; behold, here is the place where they laid Him.

"But go, tell His disciples and Peter, 'He is going ahead of you to Galilee; there you will see Him, just as He told you.' "

They went out and fled from the tomb, for trembling and astonishment had gripped them; and they said nothing to anyone, for they were afraid. *Mark 16:1-8*

An **angel** of the Lord appeared to him, standing to the right of the altar of incense. Zacharias was troubled when he saw the **angel**, and fear gripped him.

But the **angel** said to him, "Do not be afraid, Zacharias, for your petition has been heard, and your wife Elizabeth will bear you a son, and you will give him the name John.

"You will have joy and gladness, and many will rejoice at his birth. For he will be great in the sight of the Lord; and he will drink no wine or liquor, and he will be filled with the Holy Spirit while yet in his mother's womb.

"And he will turn many of the sons of Israel back to the Lord their God. It is he who will go as a forerunner before Him in the spirit and power of Elijah, to turn the hearts of the fathers back to the children, and the disobedient to the attitude of the righteous, so as to make ready a people prepared for the Lord." *Luke 1:11-22 > continued*

Zacharias said to the **angel**, "How will I know this for certain? For I am an old man and my wife is advanced in years."

The **angel** answered and said to him, "I am Gabriel, who stands in the presence of God, and I have been sent to speak to you and to bring you this good news.

"And behold, you shall be silent and unable to speak until the day when these things take place, because you did not believe my words, which will be fulfilled in their proper time."

The people were waiting for Zacharias, and were wondering at his delay in the temple. But when he came out, he was unable to speak to them; and they realized that he had seen a vision in the temple; and he kept making signs to them, and remained mute.   *> Luke 1:11-22*

In the sixth month the **angel** Gabriel was sent from God to a city in Galilee called Nazareth, to a virgin engaged to a man whose name was Joseph, of the descendants of David; and the virgin's name was Mary.

And coming in, he said to her, "Greetings, favored one! The Lord is with you." But she was very perplexed at this statement, and kept pondering what kind of salutation this was.

The **angel** said to her, "Do not be afraid, Mary; for you have found favor with God.

"And behold, you will conceive in your womb and bear a son, and you shall name Him Jesus. He will be great and will be called the Son of the Most High; and the Lord God will give Him the throne of His father David; and He will reign over the house of Jacob forever, and His kingdom will have no end."

Mary said to the **angel**, "How can this be, since I am a virgin?"

The **angel** answered and said to her, "The Holy Spirit will come upon you, and the power of the Most High will overshadow you; and for that reason the holy Child shall be called the Son of God.

"And behold, even your relative Elizabeth has also conceived a son in her old age; and she who was called barren is now in her sixth month. For nothing will be impossible with God."

And Mary said, "Behold, the bond-slave of the Lord; may it be done to me according to your word."

And the **angel** departed from her.   *Luke 1:26-38*

In the same region there were some shepherds staying out in the fields and keeping watch over their flock by night. And an **angel** of the Lord suddenly stood before them, and the glory of the Lord shone around them; and they were terribly frightened.

But the **angel** said to them, "Do not be afraid; for behold, I bring you good news of great joy which will be for all the people; for today in the city of David there has been born for you a Savior, who is Christ the

Lord. This will be a sign for you: you will find a baby wrapped in cloths and lying in a manger."

And suddenly there appeared with the **angel** a multitude of the heavenly host praising God and saying, "Glory to God in the highest, and on earth peace among men with whom He is pleased."

When the **angels** had gone away from them into heaven, the shepherds began saying to one another, "Let us go straight to Bethlehem then, and see this thing that has happened which the Lord has made known to us." So they came in a hurry and found their way to Mary and Joseph, and the baby as He lay in the manger.

When they had seen this, they made known the statement which had been told them about this Child.

And all who heard it wondered at the things which were told them by the shepherds. But Mary treasured all these things, pondering them in her heart.

The shepherds went back, glorifying and praising God for all that they had heard and seen, just as had been told them.

And when eight days had passed, before His circumcision, His name was then called Jesus, the name given by the **angel** before He was conceived in the womb.   *Luke 2:8-21*

The devil said to [Jesus], "I will give You all this domain and its glory; for it has been handed over to me, and I give it to whomever I wish. Therefore if You worship before me, it shall all be Yours."

Jesus answered him, "It is written, 'You shall worship the Lord your God and serve Him only.' "

And he led Him to Jerusalem and had Him stand on the pinnacle of the temple, and said to Him, "If You are the Son of God, throw Yourself down from here; for it is written, 'He will command His **angels** concerning You to guard You,' and, 'On their hands they will bear You up, so that You will not strike Your foot against a stone.' "

And Jesus answered and said to him, "It is said, 'You shall not put the Lord your God to the test.' "

When the devil had finished every temptation, he left Him until an opportune time.   *Luke 4:6-13*

{Jesus} was saying to them all, "If anyone wishes to come after Me, he must deny himself, and take up his cross daily and follow Me. For whoever wishes to save his life will lose it, but whoever loses his life for My sake, he is the one who will save it. For what is a man profited if he gains the whole world, and loses or forfeits himself?

"For whoever is ashamed of Me and My words, the Son of Man will be ashamed of him when He comes in His glory, and the glory of the Father and of the holy **angels**."   *Luke 9:23-26*

I say to you, everyone who confesses Me before men, the Son of Man will confess him also before the **angels** of God; but he who denies Me before men will be denied before the **angels** of God. *Luke 12:8-9*

All the tax collectors and the sinners were coming near Him to listen to Him. Both the Pharisees and the scribes began to grumble, saying, "This man receives sinners and eats with them."

So He told them this parable, saying, "What man among you, if he has a hundred sheep and has lost one of them, does not leave the ninety-nine in the open pasture and go after the one which is lost until he finds it? When he has found it, he lays it on his shoulders, rejoicing. And when he comes home, he calls together his friends and his neighbors, saying to them, 'Rejoice with me, for I have found my sheep which was lost!'

"I tell you that in the same way, there will be more joy in heaven over one sinner who repents than over ninety-nine righteous persons who need no repentance.

"Or what woman, if she has ten silver coins and loses one coin, does not light a lamp and sweep the house and search carefully until she finds it? When she has found it, she calls together her friends and neighbors, saying, 'Rejoice with me, for I have found the coin which I had lost!'

"In the same way, I tell you, there is joy in the presence of the **angels** of God over one sinner who repents." *Luke 15:3-10*

There was a rich man, and he habitually dressed in purple and fine linen, joyously living in splendor every day. And a poor man named Lazarus was laid at his gate, covered with sores, and longing to be fed with the crumbs which were falling from the rich man's table; besides, even the dogs were coming and licking his sores.

Now the poor man died and was carried away by the **angels** to Abraham's bosom; and the rich man also died and was buried.

In Hades he lifted up his eyes, being in torment, and saw Abraham far away and Lazarus in his bosom. And he cried out and said, "Father Abraham, have mercy on me, and send Lazarus so that he may dip the tip of his finger in water and cool off my tongue, for I am in agony in this flame." *Luke 16:19-24*

There came to Him some of the Sadducees (who say that there is no resurrection), and they questioned Him, saying, "Teacher, Moses wrote for us that if a man's brother dies, having a wife, and he is childless, his brother should marry the wife and raise up children to his brother.

"Now there were seven brothers; and the first took a wife and died childless; and the second and the third married her; and in the same way all seven died, leaving no children. Finally the woman died also. In the resurrection therefore, which one's wife will she be? For all seven had married her."

Jesus said to them, "The sons of this age marry and are given in marriage, but those who are considered worthy to attain to that age and the resurrection from the dead, neither marry nor are given in marriage; for they cannot even die anymore, because they are like **angels**, and are **sons of God**, being sons of the resurrection."   *Luke 20:27-36*

He came out and proceeded as was His custom to the Mount of Olives; and the disciples also followed Him.

When He arrived at the place, He said to them, "Pray that you may not enter into temptation."

And He withdrew from them about a stone's throw, and He knelt down and began to pray, saying, "Father, if You are willing, remove this cup from Me; yet not My will, but Yours be done."

Now an **angel** from heaven appeared to Him, strengthening Him. And being in agony He was praying very fervently; and His sweat became like drops of blood, falling down upon the ground.   *Luke 22:39-44*

On the first day of the week, at early dawn, they came to the tomb bringing the spices which they had prepared. And they found the stone rolled away from the tomb, but when they entered, they did not find the body of the Lord Jesus.

While they were perplexed about this, behold, two men suddenly stood near them in dazzling clothing; and as the women were terrified and bowed their faces to the ground, the men said to them, "Why do you seek the living One among the dead? He is not here, but He has risen.

"Remember how He spoke to you while He was still in Galilee, saying that the Son of Man must be delivered into the hands of sinful men, and be crucified, and the third day rise again."

And they remembered His words, and returned from the tomb and reported all these things to the eleven and to all the rest.   *Luke 24:1-9*

Some women among us amazed us. When they were at the tomb early in the morning, and did not find His body, they came, saying that they had also seen a vision of **angels** who said that He was alive.

Luke 24:22-23

Jesus saw Nathanael coming to Him, and said of him, "Behold, an Israelite indeed, in whom there is no deceit!"

Nathanael said to Him, "How do You know me?"

Jesus answered and said to him, "Before Philip called you, when you were under the fig tree, I saw you."

Nathanael answered Him, "Rabbi, You are the Son of God; You are the King of Israel."

Jesus answered and said to him, "Because I said to you that I saw you under the fig tree, do you believe? You will see greater things than these."

And He said to him, "Truly, truly, I say to you, you will see the heavens opened and the **angels** of God ascending and descending on the Son of Man." *John 1:47-51*

There is in Jerusalem by the sheep gate a pool, which is called in Hebrew Bethesda, having five porticoes. In these lay a multitude of those who were sick, blind, lame, and withered, [waiting for the moving of the waters; for an **angel** of the Lord went down at certain seasons into the pool and stirred up the water; whoever then first, after the stirring up of the water, stepped in was made well from whatever disease with which he was afflicted.] *John 5:2-4*

"Now My soul has become troubled; and what shall I say, 'Father, save Me from this hour'? But for this purpose I came to this hour. Father, glorify Your name."

Then a voice came out of heaven: "I have both glorified it, and will glorify it again."

So the crowd of people who stood by and heard it were saying that it had thundered; others were saying, "An **angel** has spoken to Him."

Jesus answered and said, "This voice has not come for My sake, but for your sakes." *John 12:27-30*

Simon Peter also came, following him, and entered the tomb; and he saw the linen wrappings lying there, and the facecloth which had been on His head, not lying with the linen wrappings, but rolled up in a place by itself.

So the other disciple who had first come to the tomb then also entered, and he saw and believed. For as yet they did not understand the Scripture, that He must rise again from the dead. So the disciples went away again to their own homes.

But Mary was standing outside the tomb weeping; and so, as she wept, she stooped and looked into the tomb; and she saw two **angels** in white sitting, one at the head and one at the feet, where the body of Jesus had been lying.

And they said to her, "Woman, why are you weeping?"

She said to them, "Because they have taken away my Lord, and I do not know where they have laid Him."

When she had said this, she turned around and saw Jesus standing there, and did not know that it was Jesus. *John 20:6-14*

The people from the cities in the vicinity of Jerusalem were coming together, bringing people who were sick or afflicted with unclean spirits, and they were all being healed. But the high priest rose up, along with all his associates (that is the sect of the Sadducees), and they were filled with jealousy. They laid hands on the apostles and put them in a public jail.

But during the night an **angel** of the Lord opened the gates of the prison, and taking them out he said, "Go, stand and speak to the people in the temple the whole message of this Life."

Upon hearing this, they entered into the temple about daybreak and began to teach.

Now when the high priest and his associates came, they called the Council together, even all the Senate of the sons of Israel, and sent orders to the prison house for them to be brought.

But the officers who came did not find them in the prison; and they returned and reported back, saying, "We found the prison house locked quite securely and the guards standing at the doors; but when we had opened up, we found no one inside." *Acts 5:16-23*

They stirred up the people, the elders and the scribes, and they came up to him and dragged him away and brought him before the Council.

They put forward false witnesses who said, "This man incessantly speaks against this holy place and the Law; for we have heard him say that this Nazarene, Jesus, will destroy this place and alter the customs which Moses handed down to us."

And fixing their gaze on him, all who were sitting in the Council saw his face like the face of an **angel**. *Acts 6:12-15*

After forty years had passed, an **angel** appeared to him in the wilderness of Mount Sinai, in the flame of a burning thorn bush. When Moses saw it, he marveled at the sight; and as he approached to look more closely, there came the voice of the Lord: "I am the God of your fathers, the God of Abraham and Isaac and Jacob." Moses shook with fear and would not venture to look.

But the Lord said to him, "Take off the sandals from your feet, for the place on which you are standing is holy ground.

Acts 7:30-40 > continued

"I have certainly seen the oppression of My people in Egypt and have heard their groans, and I have come down to rescue them; come now, and I will send you to Egypt."

This Moses whom they disowned, saying, "Who made you a ruler and a judge?" is the one whom God sent to be both a ruler and a deliverer with the help of the **angel** who appeared to him in the thorn bush.

This man led them out, performing wonders and signs in the land of Egypt and in the Red Sea and in the wilderness for forty years. This is the Moses who said to the sons of Israel, "God will raise up for you a prophet like me from your brethren."

This is the one who was in the congregation in the wilderness together with the **angel** who was speaking to him on Mount Sinai, and who was with our fathers; and he received living oracles to pass on to you.

Our fathers were unwilling to be obedient to him, but repudiated him and in their hearts turned back to Egypt, saying to Aaron, "Make for us gods who will go before us; for this Moses who led us out of the land of Egypt - we do not know what happened to him."   *> Acts 7:30-40*

You men who are stiff-necked and uncircumcised in heart and ears are always resisting the Holy Spirit; you are doing just as your fathers did.

Which one of the prophets did your fathers not persecute? They killed those who had previously announced the coming of the Righteous One, whose betrayers and murderers you have now become; you who received the law as ordained by **angels**, and yet did not keep it.

Acts 7:51-53

When they had solemnly testified and spoken the word of the Lord, they started back to Jerusalem, and were preaching the gospel to many villages of the Samaritans.

But an **angel** of the Lord spoke to Philip saying, "Get up and go south to the road that descends from Jerusalem to Gaza." (This is a desert road.)

So he got up and went; and there was an Ethiopian eunuch, a court official of Candace, queen of the Ethiopians, who was in charge of all her treasure; and he had come to Jerusalem to worship, and he was returning and sitting in his chariot, and was reading the prophet Isaiah.

Then the Spirit said to Philip, "Go up and join this chariot."

Philip ran up and heard him reading Isaiah the prophet, and said, "Do you understand what you are reading?"

And he said, "Well, how could I, unless someone guides me?" And he invited Philip to come up and sit with him.   *Acts 8:25-31*

There was a man at Caesarea named Cornelius, a centurion of what was called the Italian cohort, a devout man and one who feared God with all his household, and gave many alms to the Jewish people and prayed to God continually.

About the ninth hour of the day he clearly saw in a vision an **angel** of God who had just come in and said to him, "Cornelius!" And fixing his gaze on him and being much alarmed, he said, "What is it, Lord?"

And he said to him, "Your prayers and alms have ascended as a memorial before God. Now dispatch some men to Joppa and send for a man named Simon, who is also called Peter; he is staying with a tanner named Simon, whose house is by the sea."

When the **angel** who was speaking to him had left, he summoned two of his servants and a devout soldier of those who were his personal attendants, and after he had explained everything to them, he sent them to Joppa. *Acts 10:1-8*

While Peter was reflecting on the vision, the Spirit said to him, "Behold, three men are looking for you. But get up, go downstairs and accompany them without misgivings, for I have sent them Myself."

Peter went down to the men and said, "Behold, I am the one you are looking for; what is the reason for which you have come?"

They said, "Cornelius, a centurion, a righteous and God-fearing man well spoken of by the entire nation of the Jews, was divinely directed by a holy **angel** to send for you to come to his house and hear a message from you."

So he invited them in and gave them lodging. And on the next day he got up and went away with them, and some of the brethren from Joppa accompanied him. On the following day he entered Caesarea.

Now Cornelius was waiting for them and had called together his relatives and close friends. *Acts 10:19-24*

Cornelius said, "Four days ago to this hour, I was praying in my house during the ninth hour; and behold, a man stood before me in shining garments, and he said, 'Cornelius, your prayer has been heard and your alms have been remembered before God. Therefore send to Joppa and invite Simon, who is also called Peter, to come to you; he is staying at the house of Simon the tanner by the sea.'

"So I sent for you immediately, and you have been kind enough to come. Now then, we are all here present before God to hear all that you have been commanded by the Lord." *Acts 10:30-33*

Behold, at that moment three men appeared at the house in which we were staying, having been sent to me from Caesarea. The Spirit told me to go with them without misgivings. These six brethren also went with me and we entered the man's house.

And he reported to us how he had seen the **angel** standing in his house, and saying, "Send to Joppa and have Simon, who is also called Peter, brought here; and he will speak words to you by which you will be saved, you and all your household."

And as I began to speak, the Holy Spirit fell upon them just as He did upon us at the beginning.   *Acts 11:11-15*

Herod the king laid hands on some who belonged to the church in or-der to mistreat them. And he had James the brother of John put to death with a sword. When he saw that it pleased the Jews, he pro-ceeded to arrest Peter also. Now it was during the days of Unleavened Bread.

When he had seized him, he put him in prison, delivering him to four squads of soldiers to guard him, intending after the Passover to bring him out before the people. So Peter was kept in the prison, but prayer for him was being made fervently by the church to God.

On the very night when Herod was about to bring him forward, Peter was sleeping between two soldiers, bound with two chains, and guards in front of the door were watching over the prison. And behold, an **angel** of the Lord suddenly appeared and a light shone in the cell; and he struck Peter's side and woke him up, saying, "Get up quickly." And his chains fell off his hands.

And the **angel** said to him, "Gird yourself and put on your sandals." And he did so. And he said to him, "Wrap your cloak around you and follow me."

And he went out and continued to follow, and he did not know that what was being done by the **angel** was real, but thought he was seeing a vision.

When they had passed the first and second guard, they came to the iron gate that leads into the city, which opened for them by itself; and they went out and went along one street, and immediately the **an-gel** departed from him.

When Peter came to himself, he said, "Now I know for sure that the Lord has sent forth His **angel** and rescued me from the hand of Herod and from all that the Jewish people were expecting."

And when he realized this, he went to the house of Mary, the mother of John who was also called Mark, where many were gathered together and were praying.

When he knocked at the door of the gate, a servant-girl named Rhoda came to answer.

When she recognized Peter's voice, because of her joy she did not open the gate, but ran in and announced that Peter was standing in front of the gate. They said to her, "You are out of your mind!"

But she kept insisting that it was so. They kept saying, "It is his **angel**."

But Peter continued knocking; and when they had opened the door, they saw him and were amazed. But motioning to them with his hand to be silent, he described to them how the Lord had led him out of the prison.

And he said, "Report these things to James and the brethren." ~

Acts 12:1-17~

On an appointed day Herod, having put on his royal apparel, took his seat on the rostrum and began delivering an address to them. The people kept crying out, "The voice of a god and not of a man!"

And immediately an **angel** of the Lord struck him because he did not give God the glory, and he was eaten by worms and died.

Acts 12:21-23

Perceiving that one group were Sadducees and the other Pharisees, Paul began crying out in the Council, "Brethren, I am a Pharisee, a son of Pharisees; I am on trial for the hope and resurrection of the dead!"

As he said this, there occurred a dissension between the Pharisees and Sadducees, and the assembly was divided. For the Sadducees say that there is no resurrection, nor an **angel**, nor a spirit, but the Pharisees acknowledge them all.

And there occurred a great uproar; and some of the scribes of the Pharisaic party stood up and began to argue heatedly, saying, "We find nothing wrong with this man; suppose a spirit or an **angel** has spoken to him?"

And as a great dissension was developing, the commander was afraid Paul would be torn to pieces by them and ordered the troops to go down and take him away from them by force, and bring him into the barracks.

But on the night immediately following, the Lord stood at his side and said, "Take courage; for as you have solemnly witnessed to My cause at Jerusalem, so you must witness at Rome also." *Acts 23:6-11*

The next day as we were being violently storm-tossed, they began to jettison the cargo; and on the third day they threw the ship's tackle overboard with their own hands. Since neither sun nor stars appeared for many days, and no small storm was assailing us, from then on all hope of our being saved was gradually abandoned. *Acts 27:18-25 >*

When they had gone a long time without food, then Paul stood up in their midst and said, "Men, you ought to have followed my advice and not to have set sail from Crete and incurred this damage and loss. Yet now I urge you to keep up your courage, for there will be no loss of life among you, but only of the ship.

"For this very night an **angel** of the God to whom I belong and whom I serve stood before me, saying, 'Do not be afraid, Paul; you must stand before Caesar; and behold, God has granted you all those who are sailing with you.'

"Therefore, keep up your courage, men, for I believe God that it will turn out exactly as I have been told.   But we must run aground on a certain island."   > Acts 27:18-25

Who will separate us from the love of Christ? Will tribulation, or distress, or persecution, or famine, or nakedness, or peril, or sword? Just as it is written, "For Your sake we are being put to death all day long; we were considered as sheep to be slaughtered."

But in all these things we overwhelmingly conquer through Him who loved us. For I am convinced that neither death, nor life, nor **angels**, nor principalities, nor things present, nor things to come, nor powers, nor height, nor depth, nor any other created thing, will be able to separate us from the love of God, which is in Christ Jesus our Lord.

Romans 8:35-39

I think, God has exhibited us apostles last of all, as men condemned to death; because we have become a spectacle to the world, both to **angels** and to men.

We are fools for Christ's sake, but you are prudent in Christ; we are weak, but you are strong; you are distinguished, but we are without honor.

To this present hour we are both hungry and thirsty, and are poorly clothed, and are roughly treated, and are homeless; and we toil, working with our own hands; when we are reviled, we bless; when we are persecuted, we endure; when we are slandered, we try to conciliate; we have become as the scum of the world, the dregs of all things, even until now.

I do not write these things to shame you, but to admonish you as my beloved children.   *1 Corinthians 4:9-14*

Does any one of you, when he has a case against his neighbor, dare to go to law before the unrighteous and not before the saints? Or do you not know that the saints will judge the world?

If the world is judged by you, are you not competent to constitute the smallest law courts? Do you not know that we will judge **angels**? How much more matters of this life?   *1 Corinthians 6:1-3*

Every man who has something on his head while praying or prophesying disgraces his head. But every woman who has her head uncovered while praying or prophesying disgraces her head, for she is one and the same as the woman whose head is shaved. For if a woman does not cover her head, let her also have her hair cut off; but if it is disgraceful for a woman to have her hair cut off or her head shaved, let her cover her head.

For a man ought not to have his head covered, since he is the image and glory of God; but the woman is the glory of man. For man does not originate from woman, but woman from man; for indeed man was not created for the woman's sake, but woman for the man's sake. Therefore the woman ought to have a symbol of authority on her head, because of the **angels**.

However, in the Lord, neither is woman independent of man, nor is man independent of woman. For as the woman originates from the man, so also the man has his birth through the woman; and all things originate from God.

Judge for yourselves: Is it proper for a woman to pray to God with her head uncovered? Does not even nature itself teach you that if a man has long hair, it is a dishonor to him, but if a woman has long hair, it is a glory to her? For her hair is given to her for a covering. But if one is inclined to be contentious, we have no other practice, nor have the churches of God.   *1 Corinthians 11:4-16*

If I speak with the tongues of men and of **angels**, but do not have love, I have become a noisy gong or a clanging cymbal. If I have the gift of prophecy, and know all mysteries and all knowledge; and if I have all faith, so as to remove mountains, but do not have love, I am nothing.
1 Corinthians 13:1-2

What I am doing I will continue to do, so that I may cut off opportunity from those who desire an opportunity to be regarded just as we are in the matter about which they are boasting. For such men are false apostles, deceitful workers, disguising themselves as apostles of Christ. No wonder, for even Satan disguises himself as an **angel** of light.

Therefore it is not surprising if his servants also disguise themselves as servants of righteousness, whose end will be according to their deeds.   *2 Corinthians 11:12-15*

I am amazed that you are so quickly deserting Him who called you by the grace of Christ, for a different gospel; which is really not another; only there are some who are disturbing you and want to distort the gospel of Christ.

But even if we, or an **angel** from heaven, should preach to you a gospel contrary to what we have preached to you, he is to be accursed! As we have said before, so I say again now, if any man is preaching to you a gospel contrary to what you received, he is to be accursed!

Galatians 1:6-9

What I am saying is this: The Law, which came four hundred and thirty years later, does not invalidate a covenant previously ratified by God, so as to nullify the promise. For if the inheritance is based on law, it is no longer based on a promise; but God has granted it to Abraham by means of a promise.

Why the Law then? It was added because of transgressions, having been ordained through **angels** by the agency of a mediator, until the seed would come to whom the promise had been made. Now a mediator is not for one party only; whereas God is only one.

Is the Law then contrary to the promises of God? May it never be! For if a law had been given which was able to impart life, then righteousness would indeed have been based on law. But the Scripture has shut up everyone under sin, so that the promise by faith in Jesus Christ might be given to those who believe.

But before faith came, we were kept in custody under the law, being shut up to the faith which was later to be revealed. Therefore the Law has become our tutor to lead us to Christ, so that we may be justified by faith. But now that faith has come, we are no longer under a tutor.

For you are all **sons of God** through faith in Christ Jesus. For all of you who were baptized into Christ have clothed yourselves with Christ. There is neither Jew nor Greek, there is neither slave nor free man, there is neither male nor female; for you are all one in Christ Jesus. And if you belong to Christ, then you are Abraham's descendants, heirs according to promise.

Now I say, as long as the heir is a child, he does not differ at all from a slave although he is owner of everything, but he is under guardians and managers until the date set by the father.

So also we, while we were children, were held in bondage under the elemental things of the world. But when the fullness of the time came, God sent forth His Son, born of a woman, born under the Law, so that He might redeem those who were under the Law, that we might receive the adoption as sons.

Because you are sons, God has sent forth the Spirit of His Son into our hearts, crying, "Abba! Father!" Therefore you are no longer a slave, but a son; and if a son, then an heir through God.

Galatians 3:17 - 4:7

I beg of you, brethren, become as I am, for I also have become as you are. You have done me no wrong; but you know that it was because of a bodily illness that I preached the gospel to you the first time; and that which was a trial to you in my bodily condition you did not despise or loathe, but you received me as an **angel** of God, as Christ Jesus Himself.

Galatians 4:12-14

Let no one keep defrauding you of your prize by delighting in self-abasement and the worship of the **angels**, taking his stand on visions he has seen, inflated without cause by his fleshly mind, and not holding fast to the head, from whom the entire body, being supplied and held together by the joints and ligaments, grows with a growth which is from God.

Colossians 2:18-19

We do not want you to be uninformed, brethren, about those who are asleep, so that you will not grieve as do the rest who have no hope. For if we believe that Jesus died and rose again, even so God will bring with Him those who have fallen asleep in Jesus.

For this we say to you by the word of the Lord, that we who are alive and remain until the coming of the Lord, will not precede those who have fallen asleep. For the Lord Himself will descend from heaven with a shout, with the voice of the **archangel** and with the trumpet of God, and the dead in Christ will rise first.

Then we who are alive and remain will be caught up together with them in the clouds to meet the Lord in the air, and so we shall always be with the Lord. Therefore comfort one another with these words.

1 Thessalonians 4:13-18

This is a plain indication of God's righteous judgment so that you will be considered worthy of the kingdom of God, for which indeed you are suffering. For after all it is only just for God to repay with affliction those who afflict you, and to give relief to you who are afflicted and to us as well when the Lord Jesus will be revealed from heaven with His mighty **angels** in flaming fire, out retribution to those who do not know God and to those who do not obey the gospel of our Lord Jesus.

These will pay the penalty of eternal destruction, away from the presence of the Lord and from the glory of His power, when He comes to be glorified in His saints on that day, and to be marveled at among all who have believed - for our testimony to you was believed.

2 Thessalonians 1:5-10

By common confession, great is the mystery of godliness: He who was revealed in the flesh, was vindicated in the Spirit, seen by **angels**, proclaimed among the nations, believed on in the world, taken up in glory.

1 Timothy 3:16

Do not receive an accusation against an elder except on the basis of two or three witnesses. Those who continue in sin, rebuke in the presence of all, so that the rest also will be fearful of sinning.

I solemnly charge you in the presence of God and of Christ Jesus and of His chosen **angels**, to maintain these principles without bias, doing nothing in a spirit of partiality.

Do not lay hands upon anyone too hastily and thereby share responsibility for the sins of others; keep yourself free from sin.

1 Timothy 5:19-22

God, after He spoke long ago to the fathers in the prophets in many portions and in many ways, in these last days has spoken to us in His Son, whom He appointed heir of all things, through whom also He made the world. And He is the radiance of His glory and the exact representation of His nature, and upholds all things by the word of His power.

When He had made purification of sins, He sat down at the right hand of the Majesty on high, having become as much better than the **angels**, as He has inherited a more excellent name than they. For to which of the **angels** did He ever say, "You are My Son, today I have begotten You"? And again, "I will be a Father to Him and He shall be a Son to Me"?

And when He again brings the firstborn into the world, He says, "And let all the **angels** of God worship Him." And of the **angels** He says, "Who makes His **angels** winds, and His ministers a flame of fire."

But of the Son He says, "Your throne, O God, is forever and ever, and the righteous scepter is the scepter of His kingdom. You have loved righteousness and hated lawlessness; therefore God, Your God, has anointed You with the oil of gladness above Your companions."

And, "You, Lord, in the beginning laid the foundation of the earth, and the heavens are the works of Your hands; they will perish, but You remain; and they all will become old like a garment, and like a mantle You will roll them up; like a garment they will also be changed. But You are the same, and Your years will not come to an end."

But to which of the **angels** has He ever said, "Sit at My right hand, until I make your enemies a footstool for your feet"? Are they not all ministering spirits, sent out to render service for the sake of those who will inherit salvation?

For this reason we must pay much closer attention to what we have heard, so that we do not drift away from it. For if the word spoken through **angels** proved unalterable, and every transgression and disobedience received a just penalty how will we escape if we neglect so great a salvation?

After it was at the first spoken through the Lord, it was confirmed to us by those who heard, God also testifying with them, both by signs and wonders and by various miracles and by gifts of the Holy Spirit according to His own will.

For He did not subject to **angels** the world to come, concerning which we are speaking. But one has testified somewhere, saying, "What is man, that You remember him? Or the Son of Man, that You are concerned about him? You have made him for a little while lower than the **angels**; You have crowned him with glory and honor, and have appointed him over the works of Your hands; You have put all things in subjection under his feet." For in subjecting all things to him, He left nothing that is not subject to him. But now we do not yet see all things subjected to him.

But we do see Him who was made for a little while lower than the **angels**, namely, Jesus, because of the suffering of death crowned with glory and honor, so that by the grace of God He might taste death for everyone.

For it was fitting for Him, for whom are all things, and through whom are all things, in bringing many sons to glory, to perfect the author of their salvation through sufferings.   *Hebrews 1:1 - 2:10*

Assuredly He does not give help to **angels**, but He gives help to the descendant of Abraham. Therefore, He had to be made like His brethren in all things, so that He might become a merciful and faithful high priest in things pertaining to God, to make propitiation for the sins of the people.

For since He Himself was tempted in that which He has suffered, He is able to come to the aid of those who are tempted.   *Hebrews 2:16-18*

For you have not come to a mountain that can be touched and to a blazing fire, and to darkness and gloom and whirlwind, and to the blast of a trumpet and the sound of words which sound was such that those who heard begged that no further word be spoken to them. For they could not bear the command, "If even a beast touches the mountain, it will be stoned."

And so terrible was the sight, that Moses said, "I am full of fear and trembling."   *Hebrews 12:18-24 > continued*

But you have come to Mount Zion and to the city of the living God, the heavenly Jerusalem, and to myriads of **angels**, to the general assembly and church of the firstborn who are enrolled in heaven, and to God, the Judge of all, and to the spirits of the righteous made perfect, and to Jesus, the mediator of a new covenant, and to the sprinkled blood, which speaks better than the blood of Abel. > *Hebrews 12:18-24*

Let love of the brethren continue. Do not neglect to show hospitality to strangers, for by this some have entertained **angels** without knowing it.
Hebrews 13:1-2

As to this salvation, the prophets who prophesied of the grace that would come to you made careful searches and inquiries, seeking to know what person or time the Spirit of Christ within them was indicating as He predicted the sufferings of Christ and the glories to follow.

It was revealed to them that they were not serving themselves, but you, in these things which now have been announced to you through those who preached the gospel to you by the Holy Spirit sent from heaven - things into which **angels** long to look.

Therefore, prepare your minds for action, keep sober in spirit, fix your hope completely on the grace to be brought to you at the revelation of Jesus Christ. *1 Peter 1:10-13*

Corresponding to that, baptism now saves you - not the removal of dirt from the flesh, but an appeal to God for a good conscience - through the resurrection of Jesus Christ, who is at the right hand of God, having gone into heaven, after **angels** and authorities and powers had been subjected to Him. *1 Peter 3:21-22*

False prophets also arose among the people, just as there will also be false teachers among you, who will secretly introduce destructive heresies, even denying the Master who bought them, bringing swift destruction upon themselves.

Many will follow their sensuality, and because of them the way of the truth will be maligned; and in their greed they will exploit you with false words; their judgment from long ago is not idle, and their destruction is not asleep.

For if God did not spare **angels** when they sinned, but cast them into hell and committed them to pits of darkness, reserved for judgment; and did not spare the ancient world, but preserved Noah, a preacher of righteousness, with seven others, when He brought a flood upon the world of the ungodly; and if He condemned the cities of Sodom and Gomorrah to destruction by reducing them to ashes, having made them an example to those who would live ungodly lives thereafter; and if He rescued righteous Lot, oppressed by the sensual conduct of unprincipled men (for by what he saw and heard that righteous man, while living among them, felt his righteous soul tormented day after day by their lawless deeds), then the Lord knows how to rescue the godly from temptation, and to keep the unrighteous under punishment for the day of judgment, and especially those who indulge the flesh in its corrupt desires and despise authority.

Daring, self-willed, they do not tremble when they revile **angelic** majesties, whereas **angels** who are greater in might and power do not bring a reviling judgment against them before the Lord. But these, like unreasoning animals, born as creatures of instinct to be captured and killed, reviling where they have no knowledge, will in the destruction of those creatures also be destroyed, suffering wrong as the wages of doing wrong.

They count it a pleasure to revel in the daytime. They are stains and blemishes, reveling in their deceptions, as they carouse with you, having eyes full of adultery that never cease from sin, enticing unstable souls, having a heart trained in greed, accursed children; forsaking the right way, they have gone astray, having followed the way of Balaam, the son of Beor, who loved the wages of unrighteousness; but he received a rebuke for his own transgression, for a mute donkey, speaking with a voice of a man, restrained the madness of the prophet.

2 Peter 2:1-16

I desire to remind you, though you know all things once for all, that the Lord, after saving a people out of the land of Egypt, subsequently destroyed those who did not believe.

And **angels** who did not keep their own domain, but abandoned their proper abode, He has kept in eternal bonds under darkness for the judgment of the great day, just as Sodom and Gomorrah and the cities around them, since they in the same way as these indulged in gross immorality and went after strange flesh, are exhibited as an example in undergoing the punishment of eternal fire.

Yet in the same way these men, also by dreaming, defile the flesh, and reject authority, and revile **angelic** majesties. But Michael the **archangel**, when he disputed with the devil and argued about the body of Moses, did not dare pronounce against him a railing judgment, but said, "The Lord rebuke you!"

But these men revile the things which they do not understand; and the things which they know by instinct, like unreasoning animals, by these things they are destroyed. Woe to them! For they have gone the way of Cain, and for pay they have rushed headlong into the error of Balaam, and perished in the rebellion of Korah. *Jude 5-15 > continued*

These are the men who are hidden reefs in your love feasts when they feast with you without fear, caring for themselves; clouds without water, carried along by winds; autumn trees without fruit, doubly dead, uprooted; wild waves of the sea, casting up their own shame like foam; wandering stars, for whom the black darkness has been reserved forever.

It was also about these men that Enoch, in the seventh generation from Adam, prophesied, saying, "Behold, the Lord came with many thousands of His **holy ones**, to execute judgment upon all, and to convict all the ungodly of all their ungodly deeds which they have done in an ungodly way, and of all the harsh things which ungodly sinners have spoken against Him."

> *> Jude 5-15*

The Revelation of Jesus Christ, which God gave Him to show to His bond-servants, the things which must soon take place; and He sent and communicated it by His **angel** to His bond-servant John, who testified to the word of God and to the testimony of Jesus Christ, even to all that he saw.

Blessed is he who reads and those who hear the words of the prophecy, and heed the things which are written in it; for the time is near.

Revelation 1:1-3

Write the things which you have seen, and the things which are, and the things which will take place after these things. As for the mystery of the seven **stars** which you saw in My right hand, and the seven golden lampstands: The seven **stars** are the **angels** of the seven churches, and the seven lampstands are the seven churches.

To the **angel** of the church in Ephesus write: The One who holds the seven **stars** in His right hand, the One who walks among the seven golden lampstands, says this: "I know your deeds and your toil and perseverance, and that you cannot tolerate evil men, and you put to the test those who call themselves apostles, and they are not, and you found them to be false; and you have perseverance and have endured for My name's sake, and have not grown weary." *Revelation 1:19 - 2:3*

To the **angel** of the church in Smyrna write: The first and the last, who was dead, and has come to life, says this: "I know your tribulation and your poverty (but you are rich), and the blasphemy by those who say they are Jews and are not, but are a synagogue of Satan."

Revelation 2:8-9

To the **angel** of the church in Pergamum write: The One who has the sharp two-edged sword says this: "I know where you dwell, where Satan's throne is; and you hold fast My name, and did not deny My faith even in the days of Antipas, My witness, My faithful one, who was killed among you, where Satan dwells."   *Revelation 2:12-13*

To the **angel** of the church in Thyatira write: The Son of God, who has eyes like a flame of fire, and His feet are like burnished bronze, says this: "I know your deeds, and your love and faith and service and perseverance, and that your deeds of late are greater than at first."
Revelation 2:18-19

To the **angel** of the church in Sardis write: He who has the seven Spirits of God and the seven **stars**, says this: "I know your deeds, that you have a name that you are alive, but you are dead. He who overcomes will thus be clothed in white garments; and I will not erase his name from the book of life, and I will confess his name before My Father and before His **angels**. He who has an ear, let him hear what the Spirit says to the churches."   *Revelation 3:1-6*

To the **angel** of the church in Philadelphia write: He who is holy, who is true, who has the key of David, who opens and no one will shut, and who shuts and no one opens, says this: "I know your deeds. Behold, I have put before you an open door which no one can shut, because you have a little power, and have kept My word, and have not denied My name."   *Revelation 3:7-8*

To the **angel** of the church in Laodicea write: The Amen, the faithful and true Witness, the Beginning of the creation of God, says this: "I know your deeds, that you are neither cold nor hot; I wish that you were cold or hot. So because you are lukewarm, and neither hot nor cold, I will spit you out of My mouth."   *Revelation 3:14 -16*

I saw in the right hand of Him who sat on the throne a book written inside and on the back, sealed up with seven seals. And I saw a strong **angel** proclaiming with a loud voice, "Who is worthy to open the book and to break its seals?"

And no one in heaven or on the earth or under the earth was able to open the book or to look into it.   *Revelation 5:1-3*

I looked, and I heard the voice of many **angels** around the throne and the living creatures and the elders; and the number of them was myriads of myriads, and thousands of thousands, saying with a loud voice, "Worthy is the Lamb that was slain to receive power and riches and wisdom and might and honor and glory and blessing."
Revelation 5:11-14 > continued

And every created thing which is in heaven and on the earth and under the earth and on the sea, and all things in them, I heard saying, "To Him who sits on the throne, and to the Lamb, be blessing and honor and glory and dominion forever and ever." And the four living creatures kept saying, "Amen."

And the elders fell down and worshiped. *> Revelation 5:11-14*

After this I saw four **angels** standing at the four corners of the earth, holding back the four winds of the earth, so that no wind would blow on the earth or on the sea or on any tree.

And I saw another **angel** ascending from the rising of the sun, having the seal of the living God; and he cried out with a loud voice to the four **angels** to whom it was granted to harm the earth and the sea, saying, "Do not harm the earth or the sea or the trees until we have sealed the bond-servants of our God on their foreheads."

And I heard the number of those who were sealed, one hundred and forty-four thousand sealed from every tribe of the sons of Israel.

Revelation 7:1-4

After these things I looked, and behold, a great multitude which no one could count, from every nation and all tribes and peoples and tongues, standing before the throne and before the Lamb, clothed in white robes, and palm branches were in their hands; and they cry out with a loud voice, saying, "Salvation to our God who sits on the throne, and to the Lamb."

And all the **angels** were standing around the throne and around the elders and the four living creatures; and they fell on their faces before the throne and worshiped God, saying, "Amen, blessing and glory and wisdom and thanksgiving and honor and power and might, be to our God forever and ever. Amen." *Revelation 7:9-12*

When the Lamb broke the seventh seal, there was silence in heaven for about half an hour. And I saw the seven **angels** who stand before God, and seven trumpets were given to them.

Another **angel** came and stood at the altar, holding a golden censer; and much incense was given to him, so that he might add it to the prayers of all the saints on the golden altar which was before the throne. And the smoke of the incense, with the prayers of the saints, went up before God out of the **angel's** hand.

Then the **angel** took the censer and filled it with the fire of the altar, and threw it to the earth; and there followed peals of thunder and sounds and flashes of lightning and an earthquake.

And the seven **angels** who had the seven trumpets prepared themselves to sound them.

The first sounded, and there came hail and fire, mixed with blood, and they were thrown to the earth; and a third of the earth was burned up, and a third of the trees were burned up, and all the green grass was burned up.

The second **angel** sounded, and something like a great mountain burning with fire was thrown into the sea; and a third of the sea became blood, and a third of the creatures which were in the sea and had life, died; and a third of the ships were destroyed.

The third **angel** sounded, and a great star fell from heaven, burning like a torch, and it fell on a third of the rivers and on the springs of waters. The name of the star is called Wormwood; and a third of the waters became wormwood, and many men died from the waters, because they were made bitter.

The fourth **angel** sounded, and a third of the sun and a third of the moon and a third of the stars were struck, so that a third of them would be darkened and the day would not shine for a third of it, and the night in the same way.

Then I looked, and I heard an eagle flying in midheaven, saying with a loud voice, "Woe, woe, woe to those who dwell on the earth, because of the remaining blasts of the trumpet of the three **angels** who are about to sound!"

Then the fifth **angel** sounded, and I saw a **star** from heaven which had fallen to the earth; and the key of the bottomless pit was given to him. He opened the bottomless pit, and smoke went up out of the pit, like the smoke of a great furnace; and the sun and the air were darkened by the smoke of the pit.

Then out of the smoke came locusts upon the earth, and power was given them, as the scorpions of the earth have power. They were told not to hurt the grass of the earth, nor any green thing, nor any tree, but only the men who do not have the seal of God on their foreheads.

And they were not permitted to kill anyone, but to torment for five months; and their torment was like the torment of a scorpion when it stings a man. And in those days men will seek death and will not find it; they will long to die, and death flees from them.

The appearance of the locusts was like horses prepared for battle; and on their heads appeared to be crowns like gold, and their faces were like the faces of men. They had hair like the hair of women, and their teeth were like the teeth of lions.

They had breastplates like breastplates of iron; and the sound of their wings was like the sound of chariots, of many horses rushing to battle. They have tails like scorpions, and stings; and in their tails is their power to hurt men for five months. *Revelation 8:1 - 9:16 > continued*

They have as king over them, the **angel** of the abyss; his name in Hebrew is Abaddon, and in the Greek he has the name Apollyon. The first woe is past; behold, two woes are still coming after these things.

Then the sixth **angel** sounded, and I heard a voice from the four horns of the golden altar which is before God, one saying to the sixth **angel** who had the trumpet, "Release the four **angels** who are bound at the great river Euphrates."

And the four **angels**, who had been prepared for the hour and day and month and year, were released, so that they would kill a third of mankind. The number of the armies of the horsemen was two hundred million; I heard the number of them. *> Revelation 8:1 - 9:16*

I saw another strong **angel** coming down out of heaven, clothed with a cloud; and the rainbow was upon his head, and his face was like the sun, and his feet like pillars of fire; and he had in his hand a little book which was open. He placed his right foot on the sea and his left on the land; and he cried out with a loud voice, as when a lion roars; and when he had cried out, the seven peals of thunder uttered their voices.

When the seven peals of thunder had spoken, I was about to write; and I heard a voice from heaven saying, "Seal up the things which the seven peals of thunder have spoken and do not write them."

Then the **angel** whom I saw standing on the sea and on the land lifted up his right hand to heaven, and swore by Him who lives forever and ever, who created heaven and the things in it, and the earth and the things in it, and the sea and the things in it, that there will be delay no longer, but in the days of the voice of the seventh **angel**, when he is about to sound, then the mystery of God is finished, as He preached to His servants the prophets.

Then the voice which I heard from heaven, I heard again speaking with me, and saying, "Go, take the book which is open in the hand of the **angel** who stands on the sea and on the land."

So I went to the **angel**, telling him to give me the little book. And he said to me, "Take it and eat it; it will make your stomach bitter, but in your mouth it will be sweet as honey."

I took the little book out of the **angel's** hand and ate it, and in my mouth it was sweet as honey; and when I had eaten it, my stomach was made bitter.

And they said to me, "You must prophesy again concerning many peoples and nations and tongues and kings." *Revelation 10:1-11*

The second woe is past; behold, the third woe is coming quickly. Then the seventh **angel** sounded; and there were loud voices in heaven, saying, "The kingdom of the world has become the kingdom of our Lord and of His Christ; and He will reign forever and ever." *Revelation 11:14-15*

There was war in heaven, Michael and his **angels** waging war with the dragon. The dragon and his **angels** waged war, and they were not strong enough, and there was no longer a place found for them in heaven.

And the great dragon was thrown down, the serpent of old who is called the devil and Satan, who deceives the whole world; he was thrown down to the earth, and his **angels** were thrown down with him.

Revelation 12:7-9

I saw another **angel** flying in mid-heaven, having an eternal gospel to preach to those who live on the earth, and to every nation and tribe and tongue and people; and he said with a loud voice, "Fear God, and give Him glory, because the hour of His judgment has come; worship Him who made the heaven and the earth and sea and springs of waters."

And another **angel**, a second one, followed, saying, "Fallen, fallen is Babylon the great, she who has made all the nations drink of the wine of the passion of her immorality."

Then another **angel**, a third one, followed them, saying with a loud voice, "If anyone worships the beast and his image, and receives a mark on his forehead or on his hand, he also will drink of the wine of the wrath of God, which is mixed in full strength in the cup of His anger; and he will be tormented with fire and brimstone in the presence of the holy **angels** and in the presence of the Lamb.

"And the smoke of their torment goes up forever and ever; they have no rest day and night, those who worship the beast and his image, and whoever receives the mark of his name." Here is the perseverance of the saints who keep the commandments of God and their faith in Jesus.

And I heard a voice from heaven, saying, "Write, 'Blessed are the dead who die in the Lord from now on!' "

"Yes," says the Spirit, "so that they may rest from their labors, for their deeds follow with them."

Then I looked, and behold, a white cloud, and sitting on the cloud was one like a son of man, having a golden crown on His head and a sharp sickle in His hand.

And another **angel** came out of the temple, crying out with a loud voice to Him who sat on the cloud, "Put in your sickle and reap, for the hour to reap has come, because the harvest of the earth is ripe."

Then He who sat on the cloud swung His sickle over the earth, and the earth was reaped.

And another **angel** came out of the temple which is in heaven, and he also had a sharp sickle. *Revelation 14:6 - 15:1 > continued*

Then another **angel**, the one who has power over fire, came out from the altar; and he called with a loud voice to him who had the sharp sickle, saying, "Put in your sharp sickle and gather the clusters from the vine of the earth, because her grapes are ripe."

So the **angel** swung his sickle to the earth and gathered the clusters from the vine of the earth, and threw them into the great wine press of the wrath of God. And the wine press was trodden outside the city, and blood came out from the wine press, up to the horses' bridles, for a distance of two hundred miles.

Then I saw another sign in heaven, great and marvelous, seven **angels** who had seven plagues, which are the last, because in them the wrath of God is finished.   > *Revelation 14:6 - 15:1*

After these things I looked, and the temple of the tabernacle of testimony in heaven was opened, and the seven **angels** who had the seven plagues came out of the temple, clothed in linen, clean and bright, and girded around their chests with golden sashes.

Then one of the four living creatures gave to the seven **angels** seven golden bowls full of the wrath of God, who lives forever and ever. And the temple was filled with smoke from the glory of God and from His power; and no one was able to enter the temple until the seven plagues of the seven **angels** were finished.

Then I heard a loud voice from the temple, saying to the seven **angels**, "Go and pour out on the earth the seven bowls of the wrath of God."

So the first **angel** went and poured out his bowl on the earth; and it became a loathsome and malignant sore on the people who had the mark of the beast and who worshiped his image.

The second **angel** poured out his bowl into the sea, and it became blood like that of a dead man; and every living thing in the sea died.

Then the third **angel** poured out his bowl into the rivers and the springs of waters; and they became blood.

And I heard the **angel** of the waters saying, "Righteous are You, who are and who were, O Holy One, because You judged these things; for they poured out the blood of saints and prophets, and You have given them blood to drink. They deserve it."

And I heard the altar saying, "Yes, O Lord God, the Almighty, true and righteous are Your judgments."

The fourth **angel** poured out his bowl upon the sun, and it was given to it to scorch men with fire. Men were scorched with fierce heat; and they blasphemed the name of God who has the power over these plagues, and they did not repent so as to give Him glory.

Then the fifth **angel** poured out his bowl on the throne of the beast, and his kingdom became darkened; and they gnawed their tongues because of pain, and they blasphemed the God of heaven because of their pains and their sores; and they did not repent of their deeds.

The sixth **angel** poured out his bowl on the great river, the Euphrates; and its water was dried up, so that the way would be prepared for the kings from the east. *Revelation 15:5 - 16:12*

The seventh **angel** poured out his bowl upon the air, and a loud voice came out of the temple from the throne, saying, "It is done."   And there were flashes of lightning and sounds and peals of thunder; and there was a great earthquake, such as there had not been since man came to be upon the earth, so great an earthquake was it, and so mighty. The great city was split into three parts, and the cities of the nations fell.

Babylon the great was remembered before God, to give her the cup of the wine of His fierce wrath. *Revelation 16:17-19*

Then one of the seven **angels** who had the seven bowls came and spoke with me, saying, "Come here, I will show you the judgment of the great harlot who sits on many waters, with whom the kings of the earth committed acts of immorality, and those who dwell on the earth were made drunk with the wine of her immorality."

And he carried me away in the Spirit into a wilderness; and I saw a woman sitting on a scarlet beast, full of blasphemous names, having seven heads and ten horns.

The woman was clothed in purple and scarlet, and adorned with gold and precious stones and pearls, having in her hand a gold cup full of abominations and of the unclean things of her immorality, and on her forehead a name was written, a mystery, "BABYLON THE GREAT, THE MOTHER OF HARLOTS AND OF THE ABOMINATIONS OF THE EARTH."

And I saw the woman drunk with the blood of the saints, and with the blood of the witnesses of Jesus. When I saw her, I wondered greatly.

And the **angel** said to me, "Why do you wonder? I will tell you the mystery of the woman and of the beast that carries her, which has the seven heads and the ten horns.

"The beast that you saw was, and is not, and is about to come up out of the abyss and go to destruction. And those who dwell on the earth, whose name has not been written in the book of life from the foundation of the world, will wonder when they see the beast, that he was and is not and will come.

"Here is the mind which has wisdom. The seven heads are seven mountains on which the woman sits, and they are seven kings; five have fallen, one is, the other has not yet come; and when he comes, he must remain a little while."   *Revelation 17:1-10*

After these things I saw another **angel** coming down from heaven, having great authority, and the earth was illumined with his glory.

And he cried out with a mighty voice, saying, "Fallen, fallen is Babylon the great! She has become a dwelling place of demons and a prison of every unclean spirit, and a prison of every unclean and hateful bird. For all the nations have drunk of the wine of the passion of her immorality, and the kings of the earth have committed acts of immorality with her, and the merchants of the earth have become rich by the wealth of her sensuality."   *Revelation 18:1-3*

They threw dust on their heads and were crying out, weeping and mourning, saying, "Woe, woe, the great city, in which all who had ships at sea became rich by her wealth, for in one hour she has been laid waste! Rejoice over her, O heaven, and you saints and apostles and prophets, because God has pronounced judgment for you against her."

Then a strong **angel** took up a stone like a great millstone and threw it into the sea, saying, "So will Babylon, the great city, be thrown down with violence, and will not be found any longer." *Revelation 18:19-21*

I saw an **angel** standing in the sun, and he cried out with a loud voice, saying to all the birds which fly in mid-heaven, "Come, assemble for the great supper of God, so that you may eat the flesh of kings and the flesh of commanders and the flesh of mighty men and the flesh of horses and of those who sit on them and the flesh of all men, both free men and slaves, and small and great."

And I saw the beast and the kings of the earth and their armies assembled to make war against Him who sat on the horse and against His army.   *Revelation 19:17-19*

I saw an **angel** coming down from heaven, holding the key of the abyss and a great chain in his hand.

And he laid hold of the dragon, the serpent of old, who is the devil and Satan, and bound him for a thousand years; and he threw him into the abyss, and shut it and sealed it over him, so that he would not deceive the nations any longer, until the thousand years were completed; after these things he must be released for a short time. *Revelation 20:1-3*

Then one of the seven **angels** who had the seven bowls full of the seven last plagues came and spoke with me, saying, "Come here, I will show you the bride, the wife of the Lamb."

And he carried me away in the Spirit to a great and high mountain, and showed me the holy city, Jerusalem, coming down out of heaven from God, having the glory of God. Her brilliance was like a very costly stone, as a stone of crystal-clear jasper.

It had a great and high wall, with twelve gates, and at the gates twelve **angels**; and names were written on them, which are the names of the twelve tribes of the sons of Israel. There were three gates on the east and three gates on the north and three gates on the south and three gates on the west. And the wall of the city had twelve foundation stones, and on them were the twelve names of the twelve apostles of the Lamb.

The one who spoke with me had a gold measuring rod to measure the city, and its gates and its wall. The city is laid out as a square, and its length is as great as the width; and he measured the city with the rod, fifteen hundred miles; its length and width and height are equal.

And he measured its wall, seventy-two yards, according to human measurements, which are also **angelic** measurements.

Revelation 21:9-17

He said to me, "These words are faithful and true"; and the Lord, the God of the spirits of the prophets, sent His **angel** to show to His bond-servants the things which must soon take place. And behold, I am coming quickly. Blessed is he who heeds the words of the prophecy of this book."

I, John, am the one who heard and saw these things. And when I heard and saw, I fell down to worship at the feet of the **angel** who showed me these things.

But he said to me, "Do not do that. I am a fellow servant of yours and of your brethren the prophets and of those who heed the words of this book. Worship God."

And he said to me, "Do not seal up the words of the prophecy of this book, for the time is near. Let the one who does wrong, still do wrong; and the one who is filthy, still be filthy; and let the one who is righteous, still practice righteousness; and the one who is holy, still keep himself holy.

"Behold, I am coming quickly, and My reward is with Me, to render to every man according to what he has done. I am the Alpha and the Omega, the first and the last, the beginning and the end."

Blessed are those who wash their robes, so that they may have the right to the tree of life, and may enter by the gates into the city. Outside are the dogs and the sorcerers and the immoral persons and the murderers and the idolaters, and everyone who loves and practices lying. *Revelation 22:6-17 > continued*

"I, Jesus, have sent My **angel** to testify to you these things for the churches. I am the root and the descendant of David, the bright morning star."

The Spirit and the bride say, "Come."

And let the one who hears say, "Come."

And let the one who is thirsty come; let the one who wishes take the water of life without cost.   *> Revelation 22:6-17*

~ End of Scriptures ~

Look for these Titles in the **Sola Scriptura Topical Bible** Series:

Angels	Miracles	Commandments
Faith	The Holy Spirit	The Sabbath
Prayer	The Church	Prison
Healing	The Kingdom	Resurrection

To see more Spiritual Symbols from the Word of God get

SOLA SCRIPTURA TOPICAL BIBLE:
<u>TOP 20 SYMBOLS</u>

Featuring 20 Important Spiritual Symbols, including:

1. **Angel** / Archangel
2. **Baptism** / Baptist
3. **Believe** / Believer
4. **Christ** + Messiah
5. **Church** + Christian
6. **Commandments**
7. **Covenant**
8. **Demon** + Evil Spirit
9. **Devil** + **Satan**
10. **Faith**
11. **Gospel** + Good News + Preach
12. **Hell** + Eternal Fire
13. **The Holy Spirit** / **Spirit** (*of God*)
14. **The Kingdom** (*of Heaven / of God*)
15. **Prayer** / Pray
16. **Resurrection** / Raise the dead
17. **Salvation** + Savior
18. **Son of God** + God's Son
19. **Son of Man**
20. **Tithe** + Tenth

Available at: solascriptura.ca

Other books by Daniel John:

★ **FIVE COLUMN** - A Complete Four Gospel Harmony and Merger

★ **The Synoptic Gospel**: *The Story of The Life of Jesus*

★ **The Red Letter Gospel**: *All The Words of Jesus Christ in Red*

Available at: synopticgospel.com